MORE COOKING SECRETS OF THE CIA

Over 100 New Recipes from America's Most Famous Cooking School

MORE COOKING SECRETS OF THE CIA

Over 100 New Recipes from America's Most Famous Cooking School

by

THE CULINARY INSTITUTE OF AMERICA

Photography by Joyce Oudkerk Pool

CHRONICLE BOOKS
SAN FRANCISCO

Library of Congress Cataloging-in-Publication Data:

Culinary Institute of America.
      More cooking secrets of the CIA : 100 favorite recipes from
America's most famous cooking school / by the Culinary Institute of
America ; photography by Joyce Oudkerk Pool.
          p. cm.
      Includes index.
      ISBN 0-8118-1863-2
      1. Cookery.   I. Title
TX714.C8314 1997
641.5—dc21   97–33978
                                   CIP

Printed in Hong Kong.

Tim Ryan, Senior Vice President, CIA
Henry Woods, Project Manager
Designed by Sandra McHenry Design
Food and prop stylist: Pouké
Photo assistant: Arjen Kammeraad

We would like to express our utmost gratitude to the people at
The Gardener in Berkeley and to Carol Hacker of Tableprop in
San Francisco for their help, support, and generosity with props.

10 9 8 7 6 5 4 3

Chronicle Books
85 Second Street
San Francisco, California 94105
www.chroniclebooks.com

The chefs who have contributed to the third season of our PBS
series, *Cooking Secrets of the CIA*, as well as to this companion
book, are the heart and soul of this project. We thank them all
and wish to publicly acknowledge their contributions here.

Mark Ainsworth
Wayne Almquist
Catherine Brandel
Elizabeth Briggs
Robert Briggs
Bill Briwa
Dan Budd
Mary Cech
Ron DeSantis, CMC
Joe DiPerri
Markus Farbinger, CMPC
Eve Felder
Bo Friberg
Peter Greweling
Tom Griffiths
James Hanyzeski, CMC
Jim Heywood
Robert Jorin
Morey Kanner
Tom Kief
Lars Kronmark
Jim Maraldo
Joe McKenna, CMPC
Ferdinand E. Metz, CMC
Henri Patey
Stacy Radin
William Reynolds
Tim Rodgers
Tim Ryan, CMC
Katherine Shepard
Fritz Sonnenschmidt, CMC
Rudy Smith
Dan Turgeon
Joe Weissenberg
Jonathan Zearfoss
Greg Zifchak

ACKNOWLEDGMENTS

The Culinary Institute of America is a private, not-for-profit educational institution committed to providing the world's best culinary, pastry, and baking arts and science education. This book and its accompanying public-television series enable us to reach millions of people who may never have the opportunity to take classes at our Hyde Park or Napa Valley campuses. We wish to express our deepest appreciation to those who have made this effort possible:

Cuisinart, our major sponsor, and its team of committed professionals, for their dedication to quality products and continuous support of the CIA and "Cooking Secrets."

Weber-Stephen Products Co., manufacturer of Weber barbecue grills and accessories, for demonstrating its generosity and belief in the CIA by becoming an underwriter.

Celebrity Cruises for exceeding expectations in its strong backing by becoming an underwriter.

Illy Café, a co-sponsor, industry leader, and visionary, for its faithful dedication to the CIA.

The Danny Kaye and Sylvia Fine Kaye Foundation, the Wine Spectator Foundation, and the J. Willard Marriott Continuing Education Center for providing ideal facilities for recording our video series.

Our talented producer, Marjorie Poore, for her creativity, drive, and commitment to the CIA, and her partner and business manager, Alec Fatalevich, for his ceaseless effort in bringing this project to fruition.

Project manager, Henry Woods, whose organizational skills, talents, and tireless efforts kept things running smoothly.

The chefs of the CIA, who shared their knowledge and experience so openly and freely.

Chef Elizabeth Briggs and her crew of student volunteers, for their boundless energy in prepping recipes and organizing *mise en place*.

The book's skillful editor, Mary Deirdre Donovan, and her assistants Sabrina Bailie and David Cohen.

The talented video production staff: Michel Bisson, Skip Thela, Alain Letourneau, and Barbara Dunn.

—*Tim Ryan, Senior Vice President*
The Culinary Institute of America

91
DESSERTS

122
INDEX

132
TABLE OF EQUIVALENTS

When it comes to cooking, we can never stop learning. One of the best ways to broaden our culinary skills and recipe ideas is to uncover the secrets of the world's leader in culinary knowledge, the Culinary Institute of America (CIA).

More Cooking Secrets of the CIA contains recipes from the third season of the popular public-television series, "Cooking Secrets of the CIA." This book gives you the chance to explore Italian, American, and Mediterranean cuisines and to prepare quick and healthful meals. You'll expand your recipe collection with fresh, flavorful dishes and menus.

Certain trends have emerged in the eating habits of Americans. We are increasingly "on the go," looking for meals that are quick and easy to prepare.

At the same time, we're more health-conscious, always looking for balanced Mediterranean-style cuisine or vegetarian dishes. You'll find those dishes and more among the recipes in this cookbook.

Through our Cooking Secrets television series and *More Cooking Secrets of the CIA*, you'll learn how to add grilling techniques and quick recipes to your culinary repertoire—from Sautéed Turkey Steak with Tomato Leek Ragout to Spicy Lamb Kabobs to Soda Bread—for everyday meals as well as for fabulous entertaining.

Although we're all watching our diets more than ever, one thing has remained constant: our appreciation for fine desserts. Perhaps as a reward for our increased interest in nutrition, we're treating ourselves to higher quality cakes, cookies, and pastries.

In this cookbook, you'll find a varied selection of treats—from heart-healthy offerings to truly luscious creations—to satisfy the dessert-lover in you.

Diversity of cuisine and cultures is evident in *everything* we offer at the Culinary Institute of America, and our public-television series, "Cooking Secrets of the CIA," is no different.

The same expertise, experience, and quality that go into the CIA's curriculum were used to develop the recipes for the series and *More Cooking Secrets of the CIA.* "Cooking Secrets" brings the CIA classroom experience into your home, with the college's internationally acclaimed team of chefs and instructors sharing their ideas and knowledge while demonstrating some of their most intriguing and popular creations.

The CIA's respect for all cuisines is also evident in its range of on-campus restaurants. When the college opened the American Bounty Restaurant at its Hyde Park campus in 1982, it set the pace for the current worldwide popularity of regional American cuisine. Also in Hyde Park are the Escoffier Restaurant, which showcases modern interpretations of classic French cuisine; the Caterina de' Medici Dining Room, which features regional Italian fare; and St. Andrew's Cafe, the flagship of the college's pioneering efforts in nutritional cooking. Most recently, the Wine Spectator Restaurant opened at the CIA's continuing-education campus in California's Napa Valley featuring the dishes of the Mediterranean prepared with the freshest ingredients.

More Cooking Secrets of the CIA continues the CIA's fifty-year-long practice of upholding the principles of quality and substance in culinary education while keeping an eye trained on the future. Everything we do at the college is built on the twin pillars of tradition and innovation: our associate and bachelor's degree programs; the comprehensive continuing education courses designed for culinary professionals at our New York and California campuses; our instructional videotapes and books. One of our most exciting new projects can be seen by pointing your browser to *www.digitalchef.com* to view a new online service, Digital Chef. An unprecedented food and beverage resource, Digital Chef provides you with access to the Web's most extensive source of interactive recipes, complete with cooking techniques, tips, and nutritional analyses.

The public television program "Cooking Secrets of the CIA" and our book *More Cooking Secrets of the CIA* are two more ways the Culinary Institute of America is carrying out its goal: to provide more opportunities for professionals and consumers alike to explore the compelling, exciting world of cooking.

So be prepared to have fun and bring delectable new creations to your table.

Starters and Side Dishes

It's the little things that count: little dishes, little meals—but never little flavors. We have gathered a collection of recipes from around the country and around the world to share with you.

Little dishes, known as *mezes* through the Mediterranean, are often the easiest way to give a lift to old standby menus for summer entertaining. Standard salads can be exchanged for crisp, refreshing alternatives. Look in produce markets and farmer's markets for ingredients such as fennel, radicchio, wild mushrooms, new potatoes, and figs.

Freshly prepared side dishes such as chelou and dirty rice, vegetables hot from the grill, and home-made breads such as soda bread or chickpea bread will round out the flavors, textures, and colors of any meal.

MUHAMMARA
Walnut and Red Pepper Spread
....

Serve this Middle Eastern spread in a small bowl garnished with a drizzle of olive oil and a sprinkle of cumin. Accompany it with flatbread, crackers, or grilled peasant bread.

MAKES 1½ CUPS

¾ cup walnuts, toasted and skinned (see note)
2 tablespoons fresh French bread crumbs, toasted (see note)
1½ teaspoons ground cumin
1¼ pounds red bell peppers, roasted and peeled (see note)
6 jalapeño chilies, roasted, seeded, and peeled (see note)
2 teaspoons pomegranate molasses
   (available in Middle Eastern markets)
2 tablespoons olive oil
1 teaspoon red pepper flakes
Salt to taste
1 tablespoon fresh lemon juice or to taste

   In a blender or food processor, grind the walnuts, bread crumbs, and cumin together. Add the peppers, chilies, and pomegranate molasses. With the machine running, drizzle in the olive oil until the mixture becomes creamy. Add the pepper flakes, salt, and lemon juice. Serve at once, or, for the best flavor, cover and refrigerate for 4 to 5 days.

TO TOAST AND SKIN NUTS: Spread nuts in a shallow baking dish or in a pie pan. Toast in a preheated 350°F oven for 5 to 8 minutes, stirring once or twice, until fragrant and lightly toasted.

   To skin, wrap the nuts in a clean cloth and let cool for 5 minutes. Rub them together inside the cloth to remove most of the skins.

TO TOAST BREAD CRUMBS: Spread the bread crumbs in an even layer in a dry skillet and swirl over medium heat until the bread crumbs turn golden brown.

TO ROAST AND PEEL PEPPERS AND CHILIES: Grill or broil the peppers and/or chilies until the skin is evenly charred. Place them in a covered dish or a plastic bag until it is cool enough to handle easily. Pull away the skin, using a paring knife if necessary to completely remove all of the skin. Cut open and remove the seeds and stem.

TZAZIKI
Cucumber-Yogurt Dip

It won't take long before you find plenty of ways to enjoy this light and refreshing spread. Tzaziki is a traditional accompaniment to falafel.

MAKES 2 CUPS

1 English cucumber, coarsely grated
1 teaspoon kosher salt
1 cup plain yogurt
1 cup Yogurt Cheese (recipe follows)
¼ to ½ teaspoon minced garlic, pureed in a mortar
2 tablespoons chopped fresh mint, or 2 teaspoons dried mint
Fresh lemon juice to taste
Salt to taste (optional)

Combine the cucumber and salt in a colander and let it drain for 15 minutes. Squeeze out the excess moisture. Put the cucumber in a medium bowl and stir in the yogurt, yogurt cheese, garlic, mint, and lemon juice. Adjust the seasoning with salt if necessary.

YOGURT CHEESE
This cheese has the consistency of cream cheese and can be salted or flavored with herbs and spices.

MAKES 4 CUPS

1 quart plain natural yogurt (no pectin or gelatin added)

Place the yogurt in cheesecloth-lined sieve in a bowl deep enough to allow 1 inch between the bottom of the sieve and bottom of the bowl. Fold the cheesecloth over the top and place a small weight on the yogurt. Refrigerate and let drain overnight.

SPICY BERBER BEAN PUREE

MAKES 2 CUPS

1 cup dried cannellini or other white beans
4 cups water
2 teaspoons salt
3 garlic cloves, slivered
¼ cup olive oil
½ teaspoon cumin seed, toasted and ground (see note)
⅛ teaspoon cayenne pepper
2 tablespoons fresh lemon juice
Crostini (see page 17)

Rinse and pick over the beans. Soak beans overnight in water to cover by several inches. Drain.

In a large saucepan, combine the beans and water. Bring to a simmer and cook until tender, about 45 minutes to 1 hour. Add the salt and garlic, and simmer for another 15 minutes. Drain, reserving the cooking liquid.

In a blender or food processor, puree the beans and a little of the reserved liquid until smooth. Add the olive oil, cumin, cayenne, and lemon juice. Adjust the consistency with the reserved bean liquid. Serve with crostini.

TO TOAST SEEDS: Spread seeds in a even layer in a dry skillet and swirl over medium heat until their aroma becomes apparent. Transfer to a baking sheet and let cool before using.

SONOMA GOAT CHEESE BAKED IN GRAPE LEAVES

....

The toasted grape leaves impart a slight olive and citrus taste to the cheese. Serve warm as an appetizer with warm toasts or lavash and olives, or offer as a cheese course.

SERVES 6

Six 2-ounce rounds fresh white goat cheese, each ½ inch thick
Coarsely ground pepper to taste
3 tablespoons extra-virgin olive oil
6 to 12 grape leaves, fresh or brined

Preheat the oven to 375°F, or light a fire in a gas or charcoal grill.

Sprinkle pepper evenly on both sides of the goat cheese rounds, pressing gently to make it stick. Drizzle the goat cheese with the olive oil and set aside in cool place for at least 1 hour.

If using brined grape leaves, trim stems, rinse the leaves thoroughly, and pat dry. If using fresh grape leaves, choose unblemished, flexible leaves and rinse them thoroughly but do not trim. Place grape leaves, top-side down, on a work surface. Center a cheese on each leaf and wrap loosely.

Bake the leaf packages on a baking sheet for 6 to 8 minutes, or grill for 2 to 3 minutes on each side.

Serve at once.

TORTILLA

Spanish Potato and Onion Omelet

....

In Spain, *tortillas* are thin omelets, similar to frittatas, typically served at room temperature. This potato and onion version can be served for breakfast or brunch, or at your next cocktail party.

SERVES 12

½ cup olive oil
3 onions, quartered and cut into ¼-inch-thick slices
Salt and freshly ground pepper to taste
4 russet potatoes, peeled, quartered, and cut into
*   ¼-inch-thick slices (about 4 pounds total)*
6 large eggs, beaten

In a 10-inch skillet over medium heat, heat the oil and add the onions. Sprinkle with salt and pepper. Cook until tender, about 15 minutes. Pour the onions and oil into a sieve over a bowl. Return the strained oil to skillet and place over medium heat.

Add the potatoes and sprinkle with salt and pepper. Cook, tossing occasionally, until lightly golden, about 10 minutes. Pour the potatoes and oil into the same sieve, reserving the oil (you should have about 1 tablespoon).

In a large bowl, combine the onions, potatoes, and eggs. Return the oil to the skillet and heat over medium-high heat. Add the egg mixture and cook until set on the bottom but still runny on the top. Cover the skillet with a flat lid or a pizza pan. Quickly invert the skillet, unmolding the cake. Return to the pan, uncooked side down, and cook until the cake is set and golden brown. The center should have a little give and the sides should be firm. Turn the cake onto a platter and let sit for 15 minutes. Cut into 12 wedges and serve at room temperature.

CHEF'S TIP: If you refrigerate this before serving, bring it back to room temperature.

SAVORY WHITE BEAN PUREE

MAKES 3 CUPS

1½ cups dried cannellini or other white beans
6 cups water
2 teaspoons salt
1 garlic clove, slivered
1 fresh thyme or rosemary sprig
3 tablespoons extra-virgin olive oil
Crostini (recipe follows)

Rinse and pick over the beans. Soak the beans overnight in water to cover by several inches. Drain.

In a large saucepan, combine the beans and water. Bring to a simmer and cook until tender, about 45 minutes to 1 hour. Add the salt, garlic, and herb sprig, and continue to simmer for 15 minutes. Remove the herb sprig and drain the beans, reserving the liquid.

In a blender or food processor, puree the beans, garlic, and oil until smooth. Adjust the consistency with the reserved liquid.

Serve with crostini.

CROSTINI

Pita bread or flour tortillas, cut into wedges, may be used instead of a baguette.

SERVES 6

1 baguette (about 24 inches long), cut into ¼-inch-thick slices
½ cup olive or safflower oil
2 tablespoons mashed garlic
Salt and coarsely ground pepper to taste

Preheat oven to 350°F. Lay the bread slices in a single layer on a baking sheet.

Combine the oil, garlic, salt, and pepper. Brush both sides of the bread with the seasoned oil. Bake until lightly browned and crisp, about 5 minutes.

FRITTO MISTO

SERVES 6

2 cups dried bread crumbs
1 teaspoon dried basil
1 teaspoon dried oregano
1 teaspoon dried parsley
½ teaspoon garlic salt
2 squid, cleaned and cut into ½-inch rings
12 sea scallops
12 shrimp, peeled and deveined
12 mushrooms, stemmed
1 eggplant, cut into sticks
2 zucchini, cut into sticks
1 cup all-purpose flour
3 eggs, beaten with 2 tablespoons water
¾ cup water
2 cups oil for deep-frying
6 lemon wedges

In a medium bowl, mix the bread crumbs, herbs, and garlic salt together. Set aside. Dredge the squid, scallops, shrimp, mushrooms, eggplant, and zucchini in turn in the flour, then dip them in the egg mixture. Shake off the excess. Dip the shellfish and vegetables into the bread crumb mixture.

In a large, heavy pot or deep fryer over medium-high heat, heat 2 inches of oil to 350°F, or until a 1-inch cube of bread browns in 65 seconds. Fry the food in batches until golden brown. Using a slotted spoon, transfer to paper towels. Keep warm in a low oven until all the food is fried. Serve at once with the lemon wedges.

SPICY LAMB KABOBS WITH GRAPES

Once the lamb is marinated, this dish can be assembled and cooked in a matter of minutes. To prepare as an entree, just double the ingredients.

SERVES 8

2 [4] tablespoons olive oil
2 tablespoons fresh lemon juice
8 [3] garlic cloves, minced
2 teaspoons chopped fresh parsley
1 teaspoon minced fresh ginger
1½ teaspoons coriander seeds
¼ teaspoon ground turmeric
1 teaspoon smoky paprika, or ½ teaspoon each paprika
   and ground chipotle chili
¼ teaspoon cayenne pepper or red pepper flakes
½ teaspoon black pepper
1 tablespoon chopped fresh oregano
Several threads of saffron   18 Lamb Chops
1 pound leg of lamb, cubed, or one 8-bone rack of lamb,
   cut into chops
1 pound seedless grapes
Salt to taste

Thoroughly combine all the ingredients except the lamb, grapes and salt. Coat the meat evenly with the mixture. Cover and marinate in the refrigerator for at least 2 hours.

Light a fire in a charcoal or gas grill. Thirty minutes before grilling, soak 8 bamboo skewers in enough water to cover and remove the lamb from the refrigerator.

Thread 3 pieces of meat and 4 grapes on each skewer. Grill for 2 to 3 minutes on each side, or until medium rare. Season with salt.

BRIKS
Savory Deep-Fried Turnovers
....

Briks are sold on the streets of Tunisia to passersby on their way to work. The wrapper is a very thin crepelike pancake called a *warka*, or sometimes simply called brik pastry. According to Paula Wolfert, no self-respecting family would permit their daughter to marry anyone who could not eat these turnovers neatly.

SERVES 6

Olive oil for deep-frying
6 warkas or Chinese spring roll wrappers (see Chef's Tips)
1 tablespoon harissa (see Chef's Tips)
6 tablespoons mashed potato
6 eggs
6 tablespoons sautéed onion
1 tablespoon capers, drained
2 tablespoons chopped fresh parsley
2 tablespoons grated Parmesan cheese
Salt to taste

In a heavy skillet over medium-high heat, heat 1½ inches olive oil to 360°F, or until a 1-inch cube of bread browns in about 60 seconds.

Meanwhile, spread 1 wrapper with ½ teaspoon of the harissa. Fold in the edges to form a square and fasten down the edges with 1 tablespoon of the mashed potatoes. Holding the wrapper in a cupped hand, break an egg into the center and add 1 tablespoon of the onions, ½ teaspoon of the capers, 1 teaspoon of the parsley, and 1 teaspoon of the cheese. Coat the outer edge of the packet with a little of the egg white. Season with salt. Carefully fold one tip of the packet over to form a triangle, and press the edges to seal.

Using a slotted metal spatula, slide the triangle into the hot oil. Spoon the hot oil over the brik as it fries. Turn the brik over and brown the other side. Using the spatula, transfer the brik to paper towels to drain briefly. Serve at once. Repeat to fill and cook the remaining wrappers.

CHEF'S TIPS: Warkas may be found in specialty foods markets. Chinese spring roll wrappers make a fine substitute.

Harissa is a sauce made from hot chilies, garlic, cumin, and other spices mixed with olive oil. It is a specialty of Tunisia and is often served with couscous.

SEARED SCALLOPS WITH BEET VINAIGRETTE

SERVES 6

10 ounces bay scallops
1½ pounds beets
1 teaspoon arrowroot
1 tablespoon cider vinegar
2 tablespoons extra-virgin olive oil
Cucumber-Dill Rice Salad (recipe follows)

Remove the muscle tabs from the scallops and blot dry. Set aside. Juice the beets. In a small saucepan, cook the juice over medium-high heat to reduce to about ½ cup. Dilute the arrowroot in a little cold water. Add to the reduced beet juice and simmer until thickened, about 1 minute. Add the vinegar to the thickened beet juice. Let cool to room temperature, then whisk in the oil. Set aside.

Heat a large cast-iron skillet or nonstick sauté pan over high heat. Add the scallops (do not overcrowd the pan) and cook on the first side for about 60 seconds, or until golden. Turn the scallops and cook on the second side until golden.

Make a ring of the rice salad, set the scallops in the center of the rice, and serve with the beet vinaigrette.

CUCUMBER-DILL RICE SALAD

SERVES 6

1 cup basmati rice
2 cups water
½ teaspoon salt
½ cup diced cucumber
⅓ cup diced tomato
2 tablespoons minced red onion
1 tablespoon chopped fresh chives
2 teaspoons chopped fresh dill
4 teaspoons cider vinegar
1 tablespoon rice vinegar

In a medium saucepan, combine the rice and water. Bring to a boil, add the salt, and reduce heat to a simmer. Cover and cook for 16 minutes, or until just tender. Remove from heat, uncover, and stir the rice with a fork to fluff.

In a medium bowl, combine the cucumber, tomato, onion, chives, dill, and vinegars. Toss until the vegetables are well coated. Gently fold the vegetable mixture into the cooked rice. Cover and refrigerate for at least 1 hour before serving.

GRILLED FIGS WRAPPED IN PROSCIUTTO

Serve this delicacy alongside grilled game meats. Figs are considered by many to be a symbol of peace and prosperity.

SERVES 6

1½ cups coarse salt
3 whole cloves
1 cinnamon stick, broken into pieces
3 star anise pods
½ teaspoon pink peppercorns
½ teaspoon black peppercorns
6 allspice berries
12 fresh ripe figs
6 slices prosciutto, each cut into 4 strips
1 teaspoon olive or walnut oil
1 tablespoon best-quality aged balsamic vinegar
Leaves from 6 fresh chervil sprigs

Light a fire in a charcoal or gas grill. Preheat the oven to 350°F.

Combine the salt, cloves, cinnamon stick, star anise, pink and black peppercorns, and allspice. Make a bed of the salt mixture in an earthenware bowl or platter and bake in the oven until warm, about 15 minutes.

Cut each fig into quarters and wrap each with a strip of prosciutto. Drizzle the figs with the oil. Grill the figs for about 1 minute, or until just heated through.

Place each fig piece in the bowl of a large spoon and arrange the spoons on the warmed salt. Drizzle the figs with balsamic vinegar and top with a few chervil leaves. Serve warm.

LITTLENECK CLAMS WITH TOMATO SALSA AND LIME

The smallest of the East Coast hard-shell clams, littleneck shells are less than 2 inches in diameter. Be sure to purchase only those with tightly closed shells and use them within 2 days.

SERVES 6

TOMATO SALSA

2 tomatoes, peeled, seeded, and chopped (see note)
2 tablespoons finely diced red onion
1 tablespoon red wine vinegar
½ jalapeño chili, seeded and minced
Kosher salt and freshly cracked pepper to taste

3 bottles good-quality lager or mild ale
6 dozen littleneck clams, scrubbed
6 tablespoons diced lime flesh
Fresh cilantro leaves for garnish

To make the salsa: Combine all the ingredients and let sit at room temperature for at least 4 hours and up to overnight.

Pour 2 bottles of the beer into a large pot. Bring to a boil, add the clams, cover, and steam until the clams open, about 5 to 7 minutes.

Pour ¼ cup of the remaining beer in the bottom of each bowl. Transfer the steamed clams to the bowls (discard any that have not opened). Spoon 3 teaspoons of the salsa and 1 tablespoon of the diced limes over each serving. Garnish with cilantro.

TO PEEL AND SEED TOMATOES: Core tomatoes and score an "X" through the skin at the bottom of each. Submerge a few tomatoes at a time in a large pot of boiling water for 15 to 30 seconds. Using a slotted spoon, transfer the tomatoes to a bowl of ice water. Drain the tomatoes and pull the skins off. Cut tomatoes in half. Squeeze or scrape out the seeds.

L E B L E B I
Tunisian Chickpea Soup
....

This soup is accompanied with several garnishes. Place them in small bowls and arrange in the center of the table so your guests may add them as they wish.

SERVES 6

1½ cups dried chickpeas (garbanzo beans)
6 cups vegetable broth (see page 61) or chicken broth, heated
1 teaspoon cumin seeds, toasted (see page 14)
½ teaspoon salt
5 garlic cloves, coarsely chopped
1 teaspoon harissa (see Chef's Tips, page 20)
2 tablespoons olive oil
1 onion, diced

GARNISH

½ cup capers, drained and coarsely chopped
2 hard-cooked eggs, coarsely chopped
One 6-ounce can tuna, drained and flaked
Ground cumin
⅓ cup harissa
½ cup thinly sliced scallions, including some of the green
Extra-virgin olive oil
2 lemons, quartered
Six ½-inch-thick slices day-old French bread,
  cut into 1-inch cubes

Rinse and pick over the chickpeas. Soak the chickpeas overnight in water to cover by several inches. Drain.

In a large pot, combine the chickpeas and broth. Bring to a boil. Reduce heat to a very low simmer and cook for 20 minutes.

In a mortar or food processor, crush the cumin seeds with the salt. Add the garlic and crush to a paste. Add the paste and harissa to the soup. Simmer for 15 to 20 minutes over very low heat, or until the chickpeas are tender. In a medium sauté pan or skillet over medium heat, heat the oil and sauté the onion until translucent. Add the onion mixture to the soup pot and cook for 15 minutes. Taste and adjust the seasoning.

To serve, put each garnish, except the bread cubes, in a small bowl. Put some of the bread cubes in bottom of each soup bowl and ladle ½ cup broth over them. Divide the chickpeas among the bowls. The garnishes may be added as desired.

C O R N A N D S Q U A S H S O U P W I T H R O A S T E D R E D P E P P E R P U R E E
....

SERVES 6

6 cups water
3 fresh basil sprigs
1 garlic head, halved horizontally
2 tablespoons butter
1 cup diced onions
2 cups diced yellow squash
3 cups fresh corn kernels (about 6 ears)
Salt and freshly ground pepper to taste
Roasted Red Pepper Puree (recipe follows)

In a stockpot combine the water, basil, and garlic. Bring to a boil, reduce heat to a simmer, and cook over medium heat for 30 minutes, skimming the surface if necessary. Strain the broth and set aside.

In a large saucepan, melt the butter over medium heat and sauté the onions until translucent, about 5 minutes.

Add the squash and cook for about 5 minutes. Add the corn, salt, and pepper. Cook over low heat for 5 minutes.

Add the garlic broth and bring the soup to a simmer. Adjust the seasoning with salt if necessary. Puree the soup and strain it through a fine-meshed sieve.

To serve, bring the soup back to a full boil. Ladle it into warmed soup bowls or plates and swirl some of the red pepper puree through each portion.

ROASTED RED PEPPER PUREE

MAKES ½ CUP

1 red bell pepper
2 teaspoons olive oil
½ teaspoon balsamic vinegar
Salt and cayenne pepper to taste

Preheat the broiler. Place the pepper under the broiler and turn as it roasts so that it blackens evenly on all sides.

Put the pepper in a small bowl and cover the bowl. Let the pepper steam for 10 minutes, then remove it from the bowl and pull off the skin. Use the back of a knife to scrape away any bits that don't come away easily. Remove the seeds, veins, and stem from the pepper. Chop the flesh coarsely.

In a blender or food processor, puree the pepper, oil, and vinegar. Add the salt and cayenne.

GRILLED RADICCHIO SALAD WITH SHAVED FENNEL AND ORANGES

Radicchio is a red-leafed Italian chicory with a slightly bitter flavor. Choose heads that have crisp, full-colored leaves with no signs of browning.

SERVES 6

¼ cup orange juice
2 heads radicchio, quartered
10 tablespoons extra-virgin olive oil
Salt and freshly ground pepper to taste
Juice of 1 lemon
2 fennel bulbs, trimmed, cored, and shaved
    (reserve the tops for garnish)
3 tablespoons minced fresh chives
3 oranges, peeled and cut into segments
Red pepper flakes to taste
6 kalamata olives, pitted and cut into thin slivers

Light a fire in a charcoal or gas grill. Refrigerate 6 plates or 1 large platter. In a small, heavy saucepan, cook the orange juice over medium heat to reduce by half. Set aside.

Coat the radicchio quarters evenly with 2 tablespoons of the olive oil and sprinkle with salt and pepper. Grill over a medium fire until they are wilted and the color has changed, about 6 minutes. Cut the radicchio into ⅛-inch strips and set aside.

Combine 4 tablespoons of the olive oil with the lemon juice to make a vinaigrette and season with salt and pepper to taste. Mix the fennel, radicchio, chives, and orange segments together. Add the vinaigrette and toss to coat evenly.

Mound the salad onto the chilled platter or individual plates and garnish with the pepper flakes, reserved fennel tops, the remaining 4 tablespoons olive oil, the black olives, and a drizzle of the reduced orange juice. Serve immediately after assembling.

New England Clam Chowder

Clam chowder was first made by New England fishermen while at sea. The most seaworthy staples, seafood and salted pork, were stewed together and served with enough crackers to thicken the soup.

SERVES 8

2 ounces salt pork, minced (about 3 tablespoons)
1¼ cups chopped onion
2 tablespoons flour
3½ cups clam broth
29 ounces shucked clams, including their liquor (about 3½ cups)
2 potatoes, peeled and diced
½ teaspoon Worcestershire Sauce
¼ teaspoon white pepper
Few drops of Tabasco sauce
2 cups half-and-half
Salt to taste
1 cup chowder crackers
2 tablespoons unsalted butter, cut into 8 cubes, for garnish

In a large, heavy pot, cook the salt pork over medium heat and cook for 3 to 5 minutes, or until most of the fat has been melted. Add the onion and cook stirring, for about 5 to 8 minutes, or until tender but not browned. Add the flour and cook for 2 to 3 minutes, stirring constantly. Gradually whisk in the clam broth. Cook the soup, stirring occasionally, until thickened and smooth, about 10 minutes.

Add the clams and potatoes to the soup and simmer until the potatoes are tender, about 20 minutes. Season with the Worcestershire sauce, white pepper, and Tabasco. Add the half-and-half and season with salt if necessary.

Serve with the chowder crackers. If desired, garnish each cup of chowder with a cube of fresh butter.

CHEF'S TIP: Chowder crackers, also known as common crackers, are considered mandatory by chowder purists. If unavailable, experiment to find a cracker that can maintain some texture in the finished soup.

FENNEL AND ORANGE SALAD

SERVES 6

2 fennel bulbs, trimmed and cored
2 oranges
1 tablespoon fresh lemon juice
2 tablespoons olive oil
1 tablespoon extra-virgin olive oil
Salt and freshly ground pepper to taste
½ cup chopped fresh parsley

Thinly slice the fennel with a sharp knife or a mandoline. Cut the skin from the orange and cut the orange into crosswise slices.

Whisk the lemon juice, olive oils, salt, and pepper together to make a vinaigrette. Reserve 2 tablespoons of the parsley for garnish. Put the fennel and remaining parsley in a bowl and toss with 3 tablespoons of the vinaigrette.

Season the orange slices with salt and pepper. Drizzle them with the remaining vinaigrette. Place the fennel and oranges on chilled plates and garnish with the reserved parsley.

ABDELLA'S CARROT SALAD

Abdella Aqueunore, a Moroccan student at the CIA, prepared this salad for his chef-instructor. It was so good, he put it on the restaurant's menu. The carrot salad may be served with Moroccan Chicken, page 71.

SERVES 8

2 pounds carrots, peeled and thinly sliced
2 garlic cloves
4 tablespoons olive oil
Juice of 1 lemon
1 tablespoon ground cumin
Small pinch of cayenne pepper
1 teaspoon chopped fresh cilantro
1 teaspoon chopped fresh parsley
2 onions, finely chopped
1 cup dates, chopped

In a medium saucepan, combine the carrots and garlic. Add water to cover by 1 or 2 inches. Bring to a simmer and cook until tender, about 5 minutes. Using a slotted spoon, transfer the carrots to a bowl.

Cook the cooking liquid over medium heat to reduce to ½ cup. Whisk in 2 tablespoons of the olive oil and the lemon juice. Pour the mixture over the carrots. Add the cumin, cayenne, cilantro, and parsley. Set aside.

Heat the remaining 2 tablespoons olive oil in a medium saucepan over medium heat. Add the onions and sauté until translucent, about 5 minutes. Add the dates and cook until the dates are softened. Toss the onion mixture with the carrots. Let cool. Cover and refrigerate for 1 to 2 hours.

TOMATO SALAD WITH WARM RICOTTA CHEESE

....

Try this unique and interesting way of serving ricotta cheese for a twist on a favorite summer treat.

SERVES 6

WARM RICOTTA CHEESE

2 pounds ricotta cheese
1 teaspoon salt
¼ cup olive oil
1 teaspoon coarsely ground black pepper

3 tablespoons finely diced shallots
3 tablespoons red wine vinegar
2 tablespoons sherry vinegar
Salt and freshly ground pepper to taste
1 fresh basil sprig
½ cup pure olive oil
½ cup extra-virgin olive oil
2 pounds red, yellow, and orange cherry and pear tomatoes
1 tablespoon chopped fresh basil

TO MAKE THE RICOTTA CHEESE: Preheat the oven to 350°F. Mix the ricotta and salt together well. Put the mixture in a small baking dish or casserole. Drizzle with the olive oil and sprinkle with pepper. Bake until browned on top and bubbling around the edges, about 20 minutes. Let sit for about 10 minutes before serving.

Meanwhile, combine the shallots, vinegars, salt, pepper, and basil sprig in a bowl; let sit for 20 minutes.

Remove and discard the basil sprig. Whisk in the olive oils. Adjust the flavor as necessary with additional vinegar, salt, and pepper.

Cut any large tomatoes into halves or quarters; leave small ones whole. Add the tomatoes to the vinaigrette and toss to coat them evenly. Divide the tomatoes among 6 salad plates. Add a spoonful of the warm ricotta to each. Scatter the chopped basil over the top of the salads.

ONION-CUCUMBER SALAD

Also referred to as "hothouse" cucumbers, English cucumbers are virtually seedless. If regular cucumbers are used, scrape out the seeds before slicing to avoid imparting a bitter flavor to your salad.

SERVES 8

2 English cucumbers
2 red onions, cut into thin slices
¼ cup extra-virgin olive oil
2 tablespoons white balsamic vinegar (see Chef's Tip)
2 tablespoons chopped fresh basil
1 tablespoon chopped fresh parsley
Salt and freshly ground pepper to taste

Peel and halve the cucumbers lengthwise and cut the pieces into crosswise slices. Toss the sliced cucumbers and onions together with the olive oil, vinegar, basil, and parsley. Season with salt and pepper.

CHEF'S TIP: White balsamic vinegar, also known as "sweet wine vinegar," is available at specialty foods markets and some supermarkets.

MOZZARELLA MARINATI CON OLIVE ASSORTITI
Marinated Mozzarella with Assorted Olives

If you have a source of cheese curd, you might want to try making your own mozzarella. But it's just as good, and a lot quicker, made with fresh mozzarella balls, known as bocconcini.

SERVES 6

2 pounds mozzarella cheese curd
1 gallon water
½ cup salt
4 teaspoons minced fresh oregano
18 kalamata olives
18 picholine olives
18 dry-cured olives
18 pieces oil-packed sundried tomatoes,
    drained (reserve oil) and halved

Cut the curd into small dice. Put the curd in a small colander. In a large stockpot, bring the water to a simmer. Add the salt and place the container in the stockpot. The curd will soften and form one smooth mass.

Remove the colander from the stockpot and drain the curd. Line a work surface with a long sheet of plastic wrap. Stretch the curd out on the sheet of plastic wrap and roll the curd up jelly-roll fashion. Twist the ends of the plastic wrap closed. Tie the mozzarella log off at 2-inch intervals using short pieces of butcher's twine to create individual balls. Remove the cheese from the plastic when ready to prepare the salad. In a large bowl, toss the cheese with the oregano, olives, and tomatoes. Drizzle some of the reserved oil over the salad. Season with salt and pepper.

GRILLED NEW POTATO SALAD WITH MUSTARD SEEDS

Because new potatoes have a crisp, waxy texture, they maintain their shape throughout cooking.

SERVES 4

16 new potatoes, about 1½ inches in diameter
¼ cup olive oil
Salt and freshly cracked pepper to taste
⅓ cup extra-virgin olive oil
¼ cup mustard seeds
¼ cup chopped fresh parsley
1 tablespoon minced garlic
2 tablespoons fresh lemon juice
6 to 16 dashes of Tabasco sauce
1 tablespoon whole-grain Dijon mustard

Light a fire in a charcoal or gas grill. In a large pot, bring salted water to a rapid boil. Add the potatoes and cook for about 15 minutes, or until they can be pierced with a fork but still offer some resistance; they should be firm but not crunchy. Drain and rinse under cold water.

Cut the potatoes in half and thread them on skewers, with the cut sides facing the same way. Coat them with oil and season with salt and pepper. Grill over a medium-hot fire for 3 to 5 minutes, or until golden brown. Place the cooked potatoes in a medium bowl. Add all the remaining ingredients and toss well. Serve warm or cold.

MIXED GREEN SALAD WITH WARM BRIE DRESSING

Brie is a soft cheese with a smooth white rind. To get the best flavor, make sure it is perfectly ripe. Press the piece you are considering to make sure it is soft yet slightly resilient to the touch. If possible, ask for a sample; it should taste buttery.

SERVES 6

6 ounces Brie cheese, cut into ¼-inch slices and rind removed
1 tablespoon olive oil
2 tablespoons chopped shallots
1 tablespoon Dijon mustard
¼ cup sherry wine vinegar
Salt and freshly ground pepper to taste
4 cups mixed salad greens (romaine, radicchio, endive, red oak, etc.)
Croutons and/or crumbled bacon for garnish (optional)

Put the Brie in a 200°F oven to soften.

Meanwhile, in a small saucepan over medium heat, heat the oil and sauté the shallots until translucent, about 3 minutes. Mix in the mustard. Remove from heat and stir in the vinegar. Return to low heat and whisk in the softened cheese until it is fully melted. Season with salt and pepper.

Toss with the greens and serve immediately. For additional texture, garnish with croutons and/or bacon bits.

CHEF'S TIP: Although this dressing is best freshly made, it can be prepared ahead of time and refrigerated. To serve, heat it in a saucepan or microwave, then mix well to blend the ingredients.

VERDURA MISTA
Sautéed Vegetables

SERVES 6

2 tablespoons olive oil
1 onion, finely diced
1 zucchini, halved lengthwise, seeded, and diced
1 fennel bulb, trimmed, cored, and diced
2 garlic cloves, minced
1 tomato, peeled, seeded, and diced (see page 22)
Salt and freshly ground pepper to taste

In a large sauté pan or skillet over medium heat, heat the oil and sauté the onion until translucent, about 3 minutes. Add the zucchini and fennel and cook until tender, about 6 to 8 minutes. Add the garlic and cook for 1 minute, or until fragrant. Add the tomato and sauté for another minute. Season with salt and pepper. Serve at once.

WATERMELON, RED ONION, AND WATERCRESS SALAD

Serve this salad when watermelons are at their peak, usually June through late August.

SERVES 6

3 tablespoons white wine vinegar
6 tablespoons vegetable oil
Salt and freshly cracked pepper to taste
3 bunches watercress, trimmed
3 cups seeded watermelon cubes
1 red onion, cut into thin slices and separated into rings
3 tablespoons pine nuts, toasted (see page 13)

Refrigerate 6 salad plates or 1 large serving platter. Whisk the vinegar, oil, salt, and pepper together.

Toss the watercress in half of the dressing and the watermelon in the other half. Divide the watercress evenly between the 6 chilled plates or platter. Place equal portions of melon in the center of the watercress. Top the salad(s) with the onion rings. Garnish with cracked pepper to taste and toasted pine nuts.

Avocado, Tomato, and Corn Salad with Aged Cheddar and Chipotle-Sherry Vinaigrette

This colorful salad makes a splash on a late-summer outdoor buffet table. Chipotle, a smoked dried jalapeño chili, adds a Southwestern flare to the dressing.

SERVES 8

4 fresh corn ears, shucked
1 small head frisée, cored
8 ounces mixed baby greens
1½ cups Chipotle-Sherry Vinaigrette (recipe follows)
2 each red and yellow beefsteak tomatoes,
    cut into ¼-inch-thick slices
4 ripe California (Haas) avocados, peeled,
    pitted, and halved (see Chef's Tip)
2 pounds red and yellow cherry and pear tomatoes,
    cut in half lengthwise
2 red onions, cut into ⅛-inch-thick lengthwise slices
8 ounces aged Cheddar cheese, crumbled into bite-sized pieces

In a large pot of salted boiling water, cook the corn until tender, about 10 minutes. Drain, rinse under cold water, and let drain again. Cut the kernels from the cob, but don't go too deeply into the cob. Use the back of a knife or a spoon to scrape the corn and milk from the cobs. Set aside.

Toss the frisée and baby greens with all but 2 tablespoons of the vinaigrette. Arrange the greens on a chilled platter or individual salad plates. Place the sliced tomatoes on the greens. Cut each avocado half into a thinly sliced fan and place on top of the toma-toes. Scatter the small tomatoes, corn, red onions, and Cheddar cheese over the salad. Drizzle the remaining vinaigrette over the salad(s), and serve at once.

CHEF'S TIP: Often avocados are sold while still hard. To ripen, place hard, unripe avocados in a brown paper bag and store at room temperature until the flesh yields slightly under pressure and becomes tender.

Chipotle-Sherry Vinaigrette

MAKES 1½ CUPS

¼ cup sherry vinegar
2 tablespoons fresh lime juice
1 tablespoon minced shallots
1 tablespoon chopped fresh cilantro
1 teaspoon chopped fresh thyme
1 tablespoon chopped fresh parsley
2 canned chipotle peppers, drained and minced
1 garlic clove, minced
1 teaspoon maple syrup
1 cup plus 2 tablespoons olive oil

In a medium bowl, combine all of the ingredients except the olive oil. Gradually whisk in the olive oil until the dressing is lightly thickened. Taste and adjust the seasoning.

CHOPPED STEAKHOUSE SALAD WITH MAYTAG BLUE CHEESE AND RED WINE VINAIGRETTE

Chopped salad is a classic steakhouse offering. Maytag blue cheese gives it a rich, savory appeal. If not available, substitute any other good-quality blue cheese. The croutons, made with roasted garlic, add a special touch to the dish.

SERVES 6

2 heads Bibb or Boston lettuce, torn into bite-sized pieces
½ red bell pepper, seeded, deveined, and diced
½ cucumber, peeled, seeded, and diced
½ tomato, peeled, seeded, and diced (see page 22)
½ celery stalk, diced
4 radishes, sliced thin
Kernels cut from 1 grilled or broiled fresh corn ear
2 tablespoons capers, drained
Red Wine Vinaigrette (recipe follows)
2 ounces Maytag blue cheese, crumbled (about ⅓ cup)
Garlic Croutons (recipe follows)

In a large bowl, combine the lettuce, pepper, cucumber, tomato, celery, radishes, corn, and capers. Add the vinaigrette, and toss until the salad is thoroughly coated. Arrange on chilled plates and scatter the crumbled cheese over the salad. Top with garlic croutons.

RED WINE VINAIGRETTE

MAKES ABOUT 1 CUP

2 tablespoons balsamic vinegar
2 tablespoons red wine vinegar
1 garlic clove, minced
1 shallot, minced
1½ teaspoons Dijon mustard
1½ teaspoons honey
¾ cup olive oil
½ teaspoon chopped fresh thyme
1½ teaspoons chopped fresh oregano
1 tablespoon chopped fresh parsley
Salt and freshly ground pepper to taste

Combine the vinegars, garlic, shallot, mustard, and honey in a bowl. Gradually whisk in the oil to make a thick vinaigrette. Add the remaining ingredients.

GARLIC CROUTONS

MAKES 3 CUPS

1 garlic head
½ cup olive oil
3 cups bread cubes

Preheat the oven to 375°F. Place the garlic on a pie tin and bake until the juices turn a deep brown, about 25 to 40 minutes.

Let the garlic cool to the touch. Squeeze the garlic from its skin into a large bowl. Whisk in the olive oil to form a paste.

Add the bread cubes to the garlic paste and toss until they are evenly coated. Place on a baking sheet, and bake, stirring once, until browned and crisp, about 10 minutes. Let cool.
CHEF'S TIP: Croutons can be made up to 1 day before serving.

MIXED GRILL OF GARDEN VEGETABLES WITH THREE MEDITERRANEAN GARNISHES

See the variations at the end of this recipe for three different ways to serve this mixed-vegetable grill.

SERVES 6

3 artichokes, trimmed
Juice of 2 lemons
3 zucchini, halved lengthwise
12 new potatoes
3 fennel bulbs, trimmed
18 baby carrots
18 asparagus stalks, trimmed
½ cup olive oil
3 tablespoons minced garlic
Salt and freshly ground pepper to taste
2 onions, cut into ½-inch-thick slices
18 mushrooms, trimmed
2 each red and yellow peppers, seeded, deveined, and cut into thirds

Bring a pot of water and half of the lemon juice to a rolling boil. Add the artichokes and set a small plate or bowl on top of the artichokes to keep them submerged. Simmer for 10 to 12 minutes, or until the stem end is easy to pierce with the tip of a paring knife. Drain, rinse with cool water, and let drain again. Cut the artichokes in half lengthwise. Scoop out the hairy purple choke.

Score the zucchini with the tines of a fork. Cook the potatoes in salted boiling water until tender, about 15 minutes. Blanch the fennel, carrots, and asparagus separately for 2 minutes, or until crisp-tender. Drain and let cool to the touch. Cut the potatoes in half. Cut the fennel into quarters and core them.

Combine the olive oil, garlic, salt, and pepper in a large bowl. Add all the vegetables, turn to coat, and let sit for 30 minutes. Light a fire in a charcoal or gas grill.

Place the vegetables over a medium fire in the order given in the ingredient list. Grill the vegetables until they begin to take on color and are cooked through.

Arrange the grilled vegetables on a platter, season with the lemon juice, and serve either hot or at room temperature.

ITALIAN GRILLED VEGETABLES: Dress 2 cups curly parsley sprigs with a dressing made from ¼ cup extra-virgin olive oil, ½ teaspoon minced garlic, 1 tablespoon fresh lemon juice, and 1 table-spoon grated Parmesan cheese. Sprinkle the parsley over the grilled vegetables.

GREEK GRILLED VEGETABLES: Top the grilled vegetables with ½ cup crumbled feta cheese and 3 tablespoons chopped fresh dill. Season with lemon juice, salt, and cracked pepper to taste.

NORTH AFRICAN GRILLED VEGETABLES: Make a char-moula sauce by mixing the following ingredients together: ¼ cup olive oil, 2 tablespoons fresh lemon juice, 3 tablespoons chopped fresh parsley, 2 tablespoons chopped fresh cilantro, 1 teaspoon minced garlic, ¾ teaspoon paprika, ½ teaspoon ground cumin, a pinch of cayenne pepper, and salt and pepper to taste. Drizzle over the grilled vegetables.

FUNGHI RIPIENO
ALLA CONTESSA
Stuffed Portobello Mushrooms

SERVES 6

6 portobello mushrooms, stemmed
3 tablespoons olive oil
3 garlic cloves, minced
8 ounces hot or mild Italian sausage, casings removed
2 cups dried bread crumbs
1 cup (4 ounces) shredded provolone cheese
¼ cup minced fresh flat-leaf parsley

Place the mushrooms in a shallow dish and drizzle with 2 tablespoons of the olive oil. Grill or broil the mushroom caps, smooth side facing the fire, for 2 to 3 minutes. Remove and reserve.

Remove the sausage from the casings. Preheat the oven to 425°F. In a medium sauté pan or skillet over medium heat, sauté the meat, stirring to break it up, until lightly browned. Add the crumbs, cheese, and parsley and mix well. Add the remaining tablespoon of olive oil and stir.

Pack the stuffing into the mushroom caps. Place in a baking dish and bake until the stuffing turns golden brown, about 12 to 15 minutes.

BRAISED ARTICHOKES WITH
LEMONS, OLIVE OIL, AND THYME

Serve these artichokes with thick slices of peasant-style bread. You wouldn't want to miss out on any of the juices.

SERVES 6

4 large fresh artichoke hearts (see note)
Juice of 1 lemon (reserve lemon halves after juicing)
¼ cup olive oil
1 bay leaf
3 garlic cloves, sliced
¼ bunch fresh thyme
8 peppercorns
Salt to taste
½ cup dry white wine
1 tablespoon chopped fresh parsley

Cut the hearts into quarters. In a medium bowl, combine the artichokes, 2 tablespoons of the lemon juice, and cold water to cover. (The artichokes may be left in this solution for up to 3 hours.) Drain just before braising.

In a medium sauté pan or skillet over medium heat, heat the oil and sauté the bay leaf, garlic, and thyme for 1 minute. Add the artichokes, lemon halves, and any remaining juice and sauté, stirring, for 30 seconds. Season with salt and add the white wine. Cover and simmer gently until the artichokes are tender, about 20 minutes. Check often and add more wine or water as necessary to prevent browning.

Add the parsley and serve warm or chilled, as a side dish or starter.

TO TRIM ARTICHOKE HEARTS: Trim the stem and cut or pull away the leaves. Use a spoon to scoop out the hairy choke, leaving the heart.

GRILLED SHRIMP WITH AROMATICS

SERVES 6

24 medium shrimp, peeled and deveined
½ cup (1 stick) butter at room temperature
2 garlic cloves, minced
¾ cup bread crumbs
½ teaspoon Spanish paprika

Preheat the broiler. Butterfly the shrimp by cutting along the outer curve of the shrimp.

Mix the butter, garlic, bread crumbs, and paprika together. Pack this mixture on top of the shrimp. Broil the shrimp until they are pink and opaque and the topping is browned. Serve at once.

CHELOU
Persian Molded Rice with Crisp Potatoes

SERVES 6

2 cups basmati rice
1 Yukon Gold potato
1 tablespoon salt, plus salt to taste
1 teaspoon saffron threads
2 tablespoons olive oil or clarified butter (see note)
3 tablespoons milk
2 tablespoons unsalted butter, melted

Preheat the oven to 350°F. Rinse the basmati rice thoroughly in cold water. Soak it in cold water to cover by several inches for 30 minutes.

While the rice is soaking, peel and slice the potato as thinly as possible using a mandoline or the slicing attachment of a food processor. Rinse thoroughly to remove all starch.

Bring a 4-quart stockpot of water to a rolling boil and add the 1 tablespoon salt. Drain the rice and add to the boiling water. Cook for exactly 6 minutes. Drain in a fine-meshed sieve and set aside.

Meanwhile, in a small dry skillet over medium heat, heat the saffron, stirring constantly, until lightly toasted and aromatic, about 1 minute. Add the milk and set aside. In a 10-inch nonstick or seasoned ovenproof skillet over medium heat, heat the olive oil or clarified butter and carefully overlap the potato slices until the bottom of the pan is covered. Season with salt.

Evenly spread the rice over the potatoes. Drizzle the saffron-infused milk and melted butter over the rice. When the potatoes are sizzling, cover the pan tightly with a lid or aluminum foil and bake for about 40 minutes, or until the potatoes are golden brown and crunchy. Loosen the rice from the sides of the pan and invert the chelou onto a warmed serving platter. Cut into wedges and serve immediately.

TO CLARIFY BUTTER: Cut unsalted butter into pieces and put them in a heavy saucepan. Melt over medium to low heat until the butter separates into layers; do not stir. Skim the foam from the butter and carefully ladle the clear butter into a clean container, leaving the solids and milky liquid at the bottom of the pan.

BATTER-FRIED ONION RINGS

This simple coating fries up light and crisp and creates an excellent contrast to the tender, juicy onions.

SERVES 6

Vegetable oil for deep-frying
1 egg
1 cup milk
1 cup all-purpose flour
1 teaspoon baking powder
Pinch of salt
4 large yellow onions, cut into ¼-inch-thick slices
   and rings separated

In a large, heavy pot or deep-fryer over medium-high heat, heat 2 inches of oil to 325°F, or until a 1-inch cube of bread browns in about 65 seconds.

Meanwhile, in a medium bowl, whisk the egg and milk together. In a small bowl stir the flour, baking powder, and salt together. Add the dry ingredients to the liquid and mix well to make the smooth batter.

Dip the onion rings into the batter. Cook the onions in the oil until golden brown, about 5 minutes. Using tongs, transfer them to paper towels to drain. Season with salt to taste and serve at once.

BAKED VIDALIA ONIONS

Vidalia onions, grown only in Vidalia, Georgia, have a mild, sweet flavor and are perfect for salads, grilling, or gentle baking as in this recipe. Vidalias are available only in the springtime, but you may substitute other sweet onions whose growing seasons range from January through September. Try Walla Walla onions from Washington state, Maui onions from Hawaii, or Oso Sweet onions from South America.

SERVES 6

6 Vidalia onions
3 teaspoons salt
1½ teaspoons pepper
1 teaspoon chopped fresh rosemary
1 teaspoon chopped fresh thyme
6 tablespoons butter
6 tablespoons balsamic vinegar

Light a fire in a charcoal or gas grill. Cut twelve 12-inch squares of aluminum foil. Peel the onions and trim the root end. Be careful to leave the core in place in order to hold each onion together as it cooks. Make 3 or 4 cuts across the top of each onion, cutting only two thirds of the way down to create 6 to 8 partially cut wedges.

Set each onion in the center of a double-layered foil square, root-end down. Sprinkle the onions with the salt, pepper, and herbs, and top each with 1 tablespoon butter. Pull the foil up over each onion, creating a pouch and leaving the top of the onion exposed. Pour 1 tablespoon vinegar into each onion.

If using a gas grill, place the onions on the top shelf over medium-high heat. On a charcoal grill, place the onions around the edge of the grill rack over a medium-hot fire. Cook the onions until they are very tender, about 1 hour.

Place each onion in an individual bowl. The onion will spread open like a flower in the bowl. Pour the juices that have accumulated in the foil pouch over the onion.

THAI JASMINE RICE

Jasmine rice from Thailand is comparable to basmati rice from India. Both are fragrant and flavorful, but with subtly different aromas.

SERVES 6

2 cups jasmine rice
4 cups chicken broth or water

Preheat the oven to 400°F. Rinse the rice thoroughly in cool water until the water is clear.

In large ovenproof saucepan, combine the broth or water and rice and bring to a boil. Cover the pot with a tight-fitting lid or aluminum foil and bake for 15 to 20 minutes, or until all the water is absorbed.

Let sit for 5 minutes and fluff with a fork before serving.

RISOTTO PANCAKES WITH WILD MUSHROOM RAGOUT

SERVES 4

1½ cups water
1 cup Arborio rice
Salt to taste
2 eggs
⅓ cup grated Parmesan cheese
1 cup hazelnuts, toasted, skinned, and chopped (see page 13)
Freshly ground pepper to taste

WILD MUSHROOM RAGOUT
4 tablespoons unsalted butter
6 ounces wild mushrooms, sliced
¼ cup dry white wine
⅓ cup heavy cream
Salt and pepper to taste

½ cup peanut or olive oil

In a medium saucepan, bring the water to a boil. Add rice and salt, cover, and simmer over low heat until all the water is absorbed, about 12 to 14 minutes.

Stir in the eggs, cheese, nuts, pepper, and additional salt, if necessary. Spoon this mixture onto a baking sheet and refrigerate until cool.

Scoop up the rice with a ¼ cup measure, form it into ¾-inch-thick pancakes, and place them on a parchment paper–lined dish. (These can be covered and refrigerated for up to 8 hours.)

TO MAKE THE RAGOUT: In a medium sauté pan or skillet, melt the butter over medium heat and sauté the mushrooms until tender, about 5 minutes. Add the wine and cook until nearly evaporated. Add the heavy cream, simmer for 2 to 3 minutes, and season with salt and pepper. Set aside and keep warm.

In a large, heavy skillet over medium heat, heat the oil until fragrant. Fry the risotto cakes in batches until golden brown on both sides, about 5 minutes total cooking time. Drain on paper towels and keep warm in a low oven until all the pancakes are cooked. Serve at once, topped with the mushroom ragout.

RISOTTO CON CHIANTI
Risotto with Chianti Wine

This rice dish has a vivid hue and a flavor to match.

SERVES 10

¼ cup olive oil
1 large onion, finely chopped
2¼ cups Arborio rice
1 bottle (1 liter) Chianti
3 cups chicken broth
5 tablespoons butter
½ cup grated Parmesan cheese
Salt and freshly ground pepper to taste

In a large, heavy saucepan over medium heat, heat the oil and sauté the onion until translucent. Add the rice and stir until all the grains are coated. Add 1⅓ cups of the wine and cook, stirring constantly, until almost all the wine has been absorbed. Repeat twice to use all the wine. This will take about 10 to 12 minutes.

Add the broth and cook until the broth has been completely absorbed by the rice, about 6 to 8 minutes. Stir in the butter, cheese, and salt and pepper, and serve at once.

SODA BREAD

This is among the simplest of breads to make. Soda bread is especially delectable when hot from the oven, wrapped in a linen cloth.

MAKES 2 LOAVES OR 24 ROLLS

4 cups cake flour
2 tablespoons baking soda
⅓ cup sugar
Pinch of salt
¼ cup vegetable shortening
3 tablespoons raisins
1 tablespoon caraway seeds
1 cup plus 2 tablespoons milk

Preheat the oven to 400°F. Sift the dry ingredients together into a large bowl. Using a pastry cutter or 2 knives, cut the shortening into the dry ingredients until the mixture resembles coarse meal. Add the raisins, caraway seeds, and milk. Mix the dough until it forms a shaggy mass.

Turn the dough out onto lightly floured board and knead for 20 seconds. Divide the dough into 2 or 24 pieces. Form each piece into a ball, pressing the seams together on the bottom. Dust the rounds with flour and lightly score a cross into the top of each with a sharp knife.

Bake loaves for 30 minutes and rolls for about 8 to 12 minutes, or until they are lightly brown and sound hollow when tapped on the bottom. Let cool on wire racks.

POIS-CHICHE
Algerian Chickpea Bread
....

The "sponge" used in this recipe gives added flavor and character to the finished bread. It must be allowed to develop over a 24-hour period for the best results.

MAKES 2 LOAVES

SPONGE

⅓ *cup unbleached all-purpose flour*
3 tablespoons water
1 teaspoon active dry yeast

1 tablespoon honey
1¾ cups water
2 packages dry yeast
2 cups unbleached flour
½ cup multi-grain flour
½ cup dark rye flour
¾ cup semolina flour
⅓ *cup whole-wheat flour*
2 tablespoons salt
1 cup cooked chickpeas (garbanzo beans), drained
½ cup grated Parmesan cheese
¾ teaspoon ground cumin
¼ teaspoon cayenne pepper

TO MAKE THE SPONGE: In a small bowl, combine the flour with the water and yeast. Stir the mixture until blended, cover, and let sit in a warm place for 24 hours.

In a bowl of a heavy-duty electric mixer, stir the sponge with the honey, water, and yeast. Let sit for 10 minutes, or until bubbly. Add the flours and mix the dough on slow speed for 4 minutes. Add the salt and mix on high speed for 10 minutes. Add the remaining ingredients and mix on high speed for 9 minutes.

To make by hand, stir the sponge, honey, water, and yeast together. Let sit for 10 minutes, or until bubbly. Whisk in the flours ½ cup at a time until the mixture is thick, then stir in the salt and the remaining flours ½ cup at a time. Turn out on a lightly floured board and knead until smooth and elastic, about 8 minutes.

Place the dough in a lightly oiled bowl, turn to coat, and cover with a damp cloth. Let rise in a warm place for 1½ hours, or until doubled. Punch the dough down and turn out on a lightly floured board. Cut the dough in half and form it into smooth balls. Cover the balls with a damp cloth and let sit on the work surface for 20 minutes.

Preheat the oven to 500°F. Using a large plate, flatten the dough balls into disks. Dust a baking sheet with a little multigrain flour and set the disks on the baking sheet. Cover them again and let the dough rise for 30 minutes.

Place the bread in the oven, mist it with water, and bake for 30 minutes, or until golden and baked through.

PITA BREAD

Contrary to the standard method of allowing bread dough to rise before shaping, these loaves are first shaped, rolled, and then allowed to rise. This simplified version lets the yeast do its best work in the oven, thus assuring a better pocket in a fraction of the time. The preheated ungreased baking sheet prevents the pitas from sticking.

MAKES 24 SMALL OR 12 LARGE PITAS

2 cups warm (105° to 115°F) water
2 envelopes active dry yeast
½ teaspoon sugar
2 teaspoons salt
5 to 5½ cups all-purpose flour

Pour the water into a large bowl. Sprinkle in the yeast, sugar, and salt. Stir to dissolve. Gradually whisk in the flour ½ cup at a time to make a smooth batter. Stir in the remaining flour ½ cup at a time until the dough pulls away from the sides of the bowl.

Turn the dough out onto well-floured board. Knead until smooth and elastic, about 5 minutes. Shape the dough into an even rectangle and cut it in half lengthwise. Divide into 24 portions for small pitas or 12 portions for large pitas. Shape each portion into a smooth ball. Place the balls on a floured baking sheet. Cover with a slightly damp towel to keep them moist as you roll them out one at a time.

On a well-floured board, gently press a dough ball flat with your palm. Using a rolling pin, roll the dough from the center to the outer edge, giving the dough a ¼-inch turn after each roll, to form a perfect circle about ¼ inch thick. A large pita will be about 5 to 5½ inches in diameter and a small one about 3½ inches in diameter. Carefully turn over the circle and smooth out any creases that might prevent a pocket from forming.

Place the circle carefully on a floured surface and cover with a clean dry towel. Repeat to roll out all the dough. Let rise in a warm place for 30 to 45 minutes.

Fifteen minutes before the dough has finished rising, preheat the oven to 500°F. Place an ungreased baking sheet on the bottom rack of the oven and heat for 2 to 3 minutes.

Place 4 small pitas or 1 large pita on the hot baking sheet. Bake until the dough is puffed and lightly browned on bottom but still white on top, about 4 minutes for small pitas and 3½ minutes for large pitas. The pitas should still be soft and flexible. If desired, flip the pitas over and bake for 1 minute to brown the second side. Be careful not to let the pitas get crisp and brittle. Remove from the oven and wrap immediately in clean dry towels until cool enough to handle. Repeat this process until all the pitas are baked.

VARIATIONS: After rolling out each circle of dough, brush the top lightly with water and sprinkle with poppy seeds or toasted sesame seeds.

MAIN COURSES

INTRODUCTION

The basic cooking techniques used in the recipes in this chapter are the same ones students at the CIA constantly seek to improve and master: chopping, sautéing, braising, frying, roasting, baking, and grilling. But this hardly means that they prepare the same recipe over and over, and neither should you.

In sampling the recipes here, whether from the heartland of America or the dunes of Morocco, you will learn another important lesson: how to combine ingredients so that individual flavors are enhanced.

Texture and color play an equally important role in the taste of a dish, and these elements are given as much emphasis as is flavor. All of these essential ingredients work together to create dishes that are both satisfying and surprising.

FALAFEL

Falafel is traditionally served in a pita pocket, garnished with chopped fresh tomatoes, sliced cucumbers, shredded lettuce, and a bit of plain yogurt flavored with chopped fresh mint.

SERVES 6

3 cups dried chickpeas (garbanzo beans)
1 cup water
4 cups olive oil
2 tablespoons all-purpose flour, plus flour for dredging
½ tablespoon baking soda
3 garlic cloves, minced
1 egg, beaten
2 tablespoons chopped fresh parsley
2 tablespoons chopped fresh cilantro
2 teaspoons ground cumin
½ teaspoon ground turmeric
½ teaspoon ground coriander
Salt and freshly ground pepper to taste

Rinse and pick over the chickpeas. Soak them overnight in water to cover by several inches. Drain.

In a large saucepan, combine the chickpeas and water to cover by several inches. Bring to a boil, reduce heat to a simmer, cover, and cook until tender, about 60 to 75 minutes. Drain and set aside.

In a large, heavy pot or deep fryer, heat the oil to 350°F, or until a 1-inch cube of bread browns in about 65 seconds.

Meanwhile, in a blender or food processor, combine the drained chickpeas, water, flour, baking soda, garlic, egg, and herbs. Season the mixture with salt and pepper. Blend until the ingredients form a coarse paste. Form the mixture into twenty-four 1-inch balls and flatten each slightly between your palms.

Dredge each falafel in flour and fry them in batches in the olive oil until they are golden brown on both sides, about 3 to 4 minutes. Keep warm in a low oven until all the falafel are fried. Drain on paper towels and serve at once.

ARUGULA, PASTA, AND PORTOBELLO SALAD

Arugula, also known as rocket, rugula, and rucola, is a peppery green that stands up well to assertive flavors, such as those found in this dish.

SERVES 4

PASTA

1½ cups all-purpose flour
⅓ cup semolina flour
2 eggs

PESTO

½ cup coarsely chopped fresh basil
1 tablespoon chopped garlic
2 tablespoons toasted pine nuts (see page 13)
1 tablespoon olive oil

2 arugula bunches
1 head baby romaine lettuce
1 head red leaf lettuce
3 portobello mushrooms, stemmed and sliced
½ cup olive oil
¼ cup balsamic vinegar
Shaved Asiago cheese for garnish

TO MAKE THE PASTA: In a medium bowl or food processor, mix all the pasta ingredients to form a stiff dough. On a lightly floured board, knead the dough until smooth, about 3 minutes. Divide the dough into 2 pieces.

Put each piece through a pasta machine until the dough is quite thin. Cut the pasta into 2-inch squares, then cut the squares into triangles. Place the triangles on a wire rack and let dry for several minutes.

TO MAKE THE PESTO: In a blender or small food processor, process the basil, garlic, and pine nuts to a paste. Add the olive oil and puree until smooth. Set aside.

Cut or tear the arugula and lettuces into 3-inch pieces. Place them in a salad bowl and keep refrigerated until you are ready to assemble the salad.

In a large pot of boiling salted water, cook the pasta for 2 to 3 minutes, or until al dente.

Meanwhile, in a large sauté pan or skillet over medium heat, heat the oil and sauté the mushrooms until tender, about 4 minutes. Using a slotted spoon, transfer the mushrooms to the bed of greens, reserving the oil in the pan.

Whisk the balsamic vinegar into the oil in the pan and pour this vinaigrette over the salad. Toss to coat the greens evenly.

Drain the pasta, transfer it to the bowl of pesto, and toss until coated. Add the pasta to the salad. Top the salad with Asiago shavings. Serve immediately.

BLACK BEAN CAKES WITH FRESH SALSA

The black beans get their "meaty" taste from smoked tomatoes, not ham hocks, to create a savory, satisfying dish.

SERVES 6

1½ cups dried black beans
4 cups Vegetable Broth (see page 61)
4 tablespoons drained plain nonfat yogurt
3 tablespoons sour cream
2 tablespoons olive oil plus ½ cup for frying
⅔ cup finely chopped onion
2 tablespoons minced garlic
¾ teaspoon cumin seeds, ground
¾ teaspoon chili powder
2 egg whites, beaten until frothy
3 tablespoons fresh lime juice
¼ cup chopped fresh cilantro
1 teaspoon salt
Cornmeal for dusting
Fresh Salsa (recipe follows)

Rinse and pick over the beans. Soak the beans overnight in water to cover by several inches. Drain. In a large saucepan, combine the beans and broth. Bring to a boil, reduce heat to a simmer, cover, and cook for 50 to 60 minutes, or until tender. The broth should reduce until it is almost completely absorbed at the end of the cooking time.

In a small bowl, mix the yogurt and sour cream until blended. Refrigerate until ready to serve.

In a medium sauté pan or skillet over medium heat, heat 2 tablespoons of the olive oil and sauté the onions and garlic until golden brown, about 8 minutes. Add the cumin seeds and chili powder and sauté for 1 minute. Add the onion mixture, black beans, egg white, lime juice, cilantro, and salt and mix well.

Remove the beans from the heat and let cool to the touch. Form into 2-inch cakes and dust lightly with cornmeal. In a large sauté pan or skillet over medium heat, heat the remaining olive oil and sauté the cakes until a crust forms on both sides, about 5 minutes total cooking time. Serve immediately with the yogurt mixture and salsa.

FRESH SALSA

MAKES 4 CUPS

2 tomatoes, seeded and finely diced
4 tomatillos, husked and finely diced
1 onion, finely diced
¼ cup fresh lime juice (about 2 limes)
1 or 2 jalapeños, seeded and finely diced
¼ cup minced fresh cilantro leaves
Salt to taste

Combine all the ingredients and let sit for 1 to 2 hours. Serve immediately, or cover and refrigerate for up to 3 days.

RED ONION TARTLETS WITH VINE LEAVES

Served warm or cold, these tartlets can be transformed into a satisfying meal with the addition of a vegetable or grain salad.

SERVES 6

CRUST

3 cups sifted all-purpose flour
¼ teaspoon baking powder
½ teaspoon salt
1 cup (2 sticks) butter
8 tablespoons cold water
2 tablespoons fresh lemon juice

FILLING

¼ cup walnut oil
2 pounds red onions, sliced thin
1 tablespoon soy sauce
2 tablespoons tomato sauce
Salt and freshly ground pepper to taste
4 eggs
1 cup heavy cream

12 bottled vine leaves, rinsed and drained, heavy stems removed.

TO MAKE THE CRUST: In a medium bowl, stir the flour, baking powder, and salt together. With a pastry cutter or 2 knives, cut in the butter until the mixture has a coarse, mealy texture. Combine the water and lemon juice and quickly stir them into the flour mixture until it forms a shaggy mass.

Transfer the dough to a lightly floured board and knead lightly once or twice. Cover the dough with plastic wrap and refrigerate.

TO MAKE THE FILLING: In a large sauté pan or skillet, heat the oil over medium heat and sauté the onions until they are golden brown, about 8 minutes. Add the soy and tomato sauces, salt, and pepper. Transfer the mixture to a shallow dish, spread it in an even layer, and let cool. In a large bowl, beat the eggs and heavy cream together. Add the onion mixture and stir to blend.

Roll the dough out on a lightly floured board to a thickness of ⅛ inch. Line a 10-inch tart pan or individual 4-inch tartlet pans with the dough. Trim the edges. Line the pastry with the vine leaves.

Pour the filling into the prepared pan(s). Place on a baking sheet and bake for 20 minutes, or until the custard is lightly set and the crust is browned. Serve warm or room temperature.

CHICKPEA AND FARRO STEW

Farro is a Tuscan wheat that is served in combination with beans, traditionally cannellini beans. In the United States it is known as spelt and can be found in most natural foods stores.

SERVES 6

Orange Oil (recipe follows)
1½ cups dried chickpeas (garbanzo beans)
Sachet: 1 bay leaf, 2 fresh thyme sprigs, 2 garlic cloves, zest of 1 orange, tied in a square of cheesecloth
½ carrot, peeled
2 teaspoons salt, plus salt to taste
Cayenne pepper to taste
¼ cup olive oil
1 cup diced onion
½ cup diced celery
½ cup diced carrots
Freshly ground pepper to taste
Farro (recipe follows)
1 tablespoon chopped fresh rosemary leaves
1 tablespoon coarsely chopped fresh flat-leaf parsley

Prepare the orange oil 24 hours in advance. Rinse and pick over the beans. Soak them overnight in cold water to cover by several inches. Drain.

In a large pot, combine the beans, sachet, and carrot half. Add enough water to cover the beans by 3 inches. Bring to a boil, reduce heat to a simmer, cover, and cook for 1 hour, or until they are starting to get tender. Add the 2 teaspoons salt and cayenne, and cook until the beans are tender. Drain the chickpeas, reserving the cooking liquid. Discard the carrot half and sachet.

In a blender or food processor, puree about two thirds of the beans with a little of the cooking liquid. Return them to the whole beans in the pot.

In a medium sauté pan or skillet over medium heat, heat the olive oil and sauté the onion, celery, and chopped carrot. Stir them into the chickpeas. Return the stew to a simmer and adjust the seasoning with salt and pepper. Ladle the stew into warm bowls, top each portion with 2 tablespoons of the farro, drizzle with orange oil, and garnish with rosemary and parsley.

ORANGE OIL

MAKES ¼ CUP

2 tablespoons pure olive oil
2 tablespoons extra virgin olive oil
4 large orange zest strips

In a small, heavy pot, heat the oils over low heat until they reach 140°F. Add the orange zest. Pour the oil into a glass jar. Cover and refrigerate for 24 hours. Remove the pieces of zest.

FARRO

SERVES 6

4 cups water
½ onion
½ carrot, peeled
1 fresh thyme sprig
1 bay leaf
1 cup whole farro (spelt)
2 teaspoons salt

Rinse the farro in several changes of cold water. Remove any black kernels.

In a medium saucepan, combine the water, onion, carrot, thyme, and bay leaf. Bring to a boil, reduce heat, and simmer for 5 minutes. Add the farro and salt. Simmer uncovered for 45 to 60 minutes. The farro should pop open and be soft enough to bite, but still be chewy.

Drain the farro. Remove and discard the vegetables and herbs.

PENNE DI RISOTTO
Penne with Mushrooms, Sage, Pine Nuts, and Prosciutto

SERVES 4

5 tablespoons olive oil
1 pound penne pasta
½ cup dry sherry
8 cups chicken broth
4 ounces mushrooms, sliced
2 cups heavy cream
Salt and freshly ground pepper to taste
4 teaspoons coarsely chopped fresh sage,
    plus 4 sage leaves for garnish
4 teaspoons pine nuts, toasted (see page 13)
4 teaspoons diced prosciutto
¼ cup grated Parmesan cheese
2 tablespoons finely diced tomato

In a large sauté pan or skillet over medium heat, heat 3 tablespoons of the oil. Add the pasta and sauté until golden brown, about 2 minutes. Add the sherry and simmer until the sherry has almost evaporated, about 3 minutes.

Add one-third of the broth and simmer until the pasta absorbs the broth, about 5 minutes. Repeat until all the broth is absorbed and the pasta is al dente, a total time of about 15 minutes.

In a large sauté pan or skillet over medium heat, heat the remaining 2 tablespoons oil and sauté the mushrooms for 6 to 8 minutes, or until tender. Add the cooked penne, the cream, salt, and pepper. Bring the cream to a boil and add the sage, pine nuts, and prosciutto. Simmer over low heat until the cream is slightly reduced, about 3 to 4 minutes. Add the Parmesan and toss to blend.

Serve in warmed bowls, garnished with the sage leaves and diced tomato.

ORECCHIETTE CON SUGO DI SALSICCIE
"Little Ears" with a Sausage Sauce

SERVES 6

½ cup olive oil
1 pound mild or hot Italian sausage, casings removed
¼ cup finely chopped onion
½ tablespoon minced garlic
½ cup dry white wine
¼ cup brandy
2 cups finely chopped fresh or canned crushed tomatoes
1 tablespoon chopped fresh rosemary
4 cups heavy cream
¼ cup peas, blanched
3 ounces mushrooms, sliced
Freshly grated Parmesan cheese for serving
1 pound dried orecchiette or other shaped pasta
Pinch of red pepper flakes

In a large sauté pan or skillet over medium heat, heat the olive oil and cook the sausage until golden brown, stirring to break it up into small pieces. Using a slotted spoon, set aside on a plate. Pour off the excess fat, leaving about ¼ inch in the pan. Add the onions and sauté until translucent. Add the garlic and red pepper flakes, and sauté until golden. Add the wine and brandy, and cook until the liquid is almost evaporated. Add the tomatoes and cook for 5 minutes.

Add the sausage, rosemary, and cream. Bring to a simmer and cook over low heat until the cream thickens slightly, about 3 to 4 minutes. Add the peas and mushrooms. Set aside and keep warm.

Meanwhile, in a large pot of salted boiling water, cook the

(recipe continues)

pasta until al dente. Drain. Add the pasta to the warm sauce and cook until heated through and coated with sauce. Serve with Parmesan cheese alongside.

CHEF'S TIPS: The sausage will probably provide enough salt for this dish. Only add salt after making sauce if you feel it is necessary. Use high-quality sausage from a good butcher. Many supermarket brands of sausage are inferior quality.

POTATO NOODLES WITH GRILLED VEGETABLES

SERVES 6

POTATO NOODLES

5 unpeeled Idaho potatoes, scrubbed
½ cup all-purpose flour
2 eggs
2 teaspoons salt
⅛ teaspoon ground nutmeg
⅛ teaspoon pepper

MARINADE

½ cup olive oil
2 tablespoons Dijon mustard
2 tablespoons lime juice
1 tablespoon minced fresh thyme
1 tablespoon kosher salt
1 tablespoon roasted garlic (see page 36)
1 tablespoon ketchup
1 teaspoon coarsely ground pepper
1 teaspoon minced fresh tarragon
1 teaspoon minced fresh flat-leaf parsley

2 red onions, quartered
2 red bell peppers, halved, seeded, and deveined
2 yellow bell peppers, halved, seeded, and deveined
2 portobello mushrooms, stemmed
3 zucchini, cut lengthwise into slices
2 yellow squash, cut lengthwise into slices
4 plum tomatoes, halved and seeded
¾ cup drained canned artichoke hearts
1 tablespoon olive oil

TO MAKE THE NOODLES: Cook the potatoes in boiling salted water until tender. Drain. While the potatoes are still very hot, coarsely shred them into a bowl using a box grater. Immediately add the flour, eggs, salt, nutmeg, and pepper. Stir until evenly blended.

Dredge your hands in flour. Break off a grape-sized bit of the potato dough. Roll the dough out to make a 3-inch-long noodle. Place on a lightly floured surface. Repeat until all the dough is rolled.

Bring a large pot of salted water to a simmer. Roll the noodles into the water and cook for about 4 minutes. Using a slotted spoon, transfer the noodles to a colander. Drain, cover, and refrigerate.

Light a fire in a charcoal grill. Twenty minutes before grilling, combine all the ingredients for the marinade in a large bowl. Add the vegetables and toss until they are evenly coated.

Let the vegetables marinate for 20 minutes. Drain, reserving the marinade. Grill the onions over a medium-hot fire until they are fully cooked and tender. Grill the peppers, skin-side down, until the skin blisters. Remove them from the grill and scrape away the charred skin. Grill the remaining vegetables until they are grill-marked and wilted. Set all the vegetables aside and keep warm.

In a large sauté pan or skillet over medium heat, heat the oil and brown the potato noodles carefully on both sides. Arrange the noodles in a warmed bowl or platter and surround them with the warm grilled vegetables. Drizzle them with some of the reserved marinade.

VEGETABLE POT PIE

Adjust the vegetables in the pie according to what's in season and enjoy it all year round.

SERVES 6

PARSNIP-POTATO DUCHESSE

1 pound potatoes, peeled and quartered
8 ounces parsnips, peeled and quartered
4 egg yolks, lightly beaten
3 tablespoons butter at room temperature
Salt to taste

6 tablespoons olive oil
8 ounces shiitake mushrooms, stemmed
Salt and freshly ground pepper to taste
1 zucchini, cut into lengthwise strips
3 carrots, peeled and cut into lengthwise strips
1 fennel bulb, trimmed, cored, and cut into sixths
4 celery stalks, peeled
1 tomato, peeled, seeded, and chopped (see page 22)
1½ cups Vegetable Velouté (recipe follows)
¼ cup chopped fresh herbs
¼ cup aged sweet wine vinegar

TO MAKE THE DUCHESSE: Bring 2 pots of water to a boil and salt the water lightly, if desired. Cook the potatoes and parsnips separately, until they are just tender, about 10 to 15 minutes. Drain.

Return the parsnips and potatoes to the pots and dry them over low heat for 2 to 3 minutes. Immediately puree the potatoes and parsnips through a food mill or ricer into a large bowl. Stir in the egg yolks, butter, and salt.

Line an 8-inch springform pan or 8-cup casserole with three-quarters of the potato mixture; reserve the rest for the crust. Preheat a grill to low heat. Preheat the oven to 350°F.

In a medium sauté pan or skillet over medium heat, heat 2 tablespoons of the olive oil and sauté the shiitakes until tender, about 3 to 4 minutes. Season with salt and pepper. Using tongs, arrange the mushrooms in a layer over the potato mixture.

Toss the zucchini, carrots, fennel, and celery in the remaining 4 tablespoons of the olive oil. Season the vegetables with salt and pepper to taste. Grill the vegetables until tender. Cut the grilled vegetables into bite-sized pieces. Add them to the velouté along with the tomato. Bring the velouté to a simmer over medium heat. Cook the filling until the vegetables are heated through. Add the herbs and vinegar. Adjust the seasoning with salt and pepper. Spoon the mixture into the prepared pan or casserole.

Put the remaining potato mixture into a pastry bag and pipe a lattice on top of the filling.

Bake for 30 to 35 minutes, or until the crust is golden brown. Let cool for 10 minutes before serving.

VEGETABLE VELOUTÉ

MAKES 3 CUPS

½ cup all-purpose flour
3 cups Vegetable Broth, heated (recipe follows)
Salt to taste

Preheat the oven to 350°F. Put the flour in a small dry sauté pan or skillet. Toast, stirring over low heat, until it is light brown. Transfer the flour to a food processor or blender. With the machine running, pour in the vegetable broth.

Pour the broth mixture into a small saucepan. Bring to a simmer over medium heat, stirring frequently. Simmer the velouté for 10 minutes, or until thickened and smooth. Season with salt.

CHEF'S TIP: To store, let cool, cover and refrigerate for up to 4 days.

CHICKEN VELOUTÉ: Follow the above recipe, substituting chicken broth for vegetable broth.

VEGETABLE BROTH

MAKES 9 CUPS

1 parsnip, chopped
1½ tomatoes, chopped
Fronds from 1 fennel bulb, chopped
1 yellow turnip, chopped
12 mushrooms
6 celery stalks, chopped
1 leek, cleaned and chopped
1 carrot, chopped
8 cups water
1 cup dry vermouth
Salt and freshly ground pepper to taste

Combine all the ingredients in a stockpot. Bring gradually to a boil over medium heat. Reduce heat to a simmer and cook for 1 hour, skimming the surface occasionally.

CHEF'S TIP: To store, let cool, cover, and refrigerate for up to 3 days, or freeze for up to 3 months.

GRILLED CHICKEN WITH HORSERADISH MARINADE

Horseradish gives grilled chicken a jolt of heat.

SERVES 6

3 boneless, skinless whole chicken breasts
1 to 2 tablespoons prepared horseradish
½ Vidalia or other sweet onion, grated
2 to 3 tablespoons balsamic vinegar
2 tablespoons olive oil
½ teaspoon juniper berries, crushed
1 teaspoon chopped fresh rosemary
2 garlic cloves, minced
Salt and pepper to taste

Trim any visible fat from the chicken breasts and cut each one in half. Place them in a shallow baking dish. In a blender or food processor, puree the horseradish, onions, balsamic vinegar, olive oil, juniper berries, rosemary, and garlic. Brush the chicken breasts with the horseradish mixture. Cover and refrigerate for 2 hours. Turn the chicken over and marinate 2 hours longer.

Light a fire in a charcoal or gas grill. Remove the breasts from the marinade and dry with paper towels. Brush with oil and season with salt and pepper. Grill over a hot fire 3 to 4 minutes on each side, or until opaque throughout. Serve at once.

STUFFED BABY PUMPKINS WITH A VEGETABLE RAGOUT

For a complete meal, serve the stuffed pumpkins with a grain like quinoa or couscous.

SERVES 6

6 miniature pumpkins
6 asparagus spears, peeled
2 carrots, peeled
2 red onions
1 Idaho potato
1 zucchini
½ cup white cultivated mushrooms

¼ cup heavy cream
1 tablespoon chopped fresh dill
1 tablespoon chopped fresh parsley
6 fresh basil leaves, chopped
1 tablespoon chopped fresh chives
4 tablespoons butter plus 3 tablespoons melted butter
Salt and freshly ground pepper to taste

Preheat the oven to 350°F. Cut lids from the pumpkins and scoop out the seeds. Place the pumpkins (including the lids) in a baking dish with ¼ cup water. Cover the baking sheet tightly with aluminum foil.

Cut the asparagus, carrots, red onions, potato, zucchini, and mushrooms into pieces. Place them on a second baking sheet with a few spoonfuls of water. Cover the pan tightly with aluminum foil.

Bake the pumpkin and cut vegetables until they are tender. The pumpkins will take about 20 minutes, the vegetables about 10 to 12 minutes.

In a small saucepan, bring the cream to a boil. Add the herbs to the cream, reduce heat, and simmer until the cream is reduced by half. Add the butter to the cream and stir to melt. Add this mixture to the roasted vegetables. Season with salt and pepper.

Ladle the vegetable stew into the pumpkin shells. Replace the lids. Brush the pumpkins all over with a little melted butter to make them shine. Reheat in the oven for 15 minutes to be sure that all of the ingredients are very hot.

GRILLED PIZZA

Whether baked or grilled, the success of any pizza relies on the quality of the dough. Ours is easy to assemble. Don't overwork it, and give the yeast plenty of time to do its job.

MAKES 10 INDIVIDUAL PIZZAS

Pizza Dough (recipe follows)
6 tablespoons olive oil
3 tablespoons chopped fresh basil
1 tablespoon chopped fresh cilantro
3 tablespoons chopped garlic
8 ounces black olives, pitted and sliced
1½ cups sliced onions, sautéed until limp
2 cups (8 ounces) shredded mozzarella
2 cups (8 ounces) crumbed feta cheese
Salt and freshly ground pepper to taste

Light a fire on one side of a charcoal grill, or preheat a gas grill to high on one side for about 20 minutes, leaving the other side cold. On an oiled grill rack on the hot side, cook 2 or 3 of the dough disks at a time for about 45 seconds. Turn the dough over on the cold side of the grill. Brush the marked side of the dough with a little oil. Scatter the topping ingredients evenly over the pizzas.

Pull the topped pizzas back onto the hot side of the grill, cover the grill, and cook for 4 to 5 minutes, or until the dough is cooked through and the cheese is browned.

PIZZA DOUGH

MAKES ENOUGH FOR TEN 8-INCH PIZZA DISKS

2 tablespoons all-purpose flour
1½ cups warm (105° to 115°F) water
1 tablespoon honey
1 package dry yeast
4 to 5 cups bread flour
½ teaspoon salt

In a heavy-duty mixer, combine the all-purpose flour, water, honey, and yeast. Mix together and let sit for 15 minutes, or until bubbly. Gradually beat in the bread flour to make a stiff dough. Knead with a dough hook for 5 minutes. To make by hand: In a large bowl, whisk the all-purpose flour, water, honey, and yeast together. Let sit for 15 minutes, or until bubbly. Gradually stir in the salt and bread flour as necessary to make a stiff dough. Turn out onto a lightly floured board and knead the dough until smooth and elastic, about 12 minutes.

Cover and let rise in a warm place for 1½ to 2 hours, or until nearly doubled in size. Punch the dough down and turn out on a lightly floured board. Divide into 10 equal pieces. Roll into balls, cover with a damp cloth, and let sit for 20 to 30 minutes. Roll each ball into a disk about 8 inches in diameter.

CHEF'S TIP: Stack the disks you don't want to grill right away between parchment paper or aluminum foil sprinkled with cornmeal. Freeze them for up to 2 months.

WHITE CHILI

Adjust the seasonings in this recipe to create your own signature "bowl of white."

SERVES 6

1 cup dried chickpeas (garbanzo beans)
1 cup dried white beans
Six 6-inch round loaves of bread
¼ cup olive oil
8 ounces ground chicken or turkey
¾ cup minced onion
3 garlic cloves, minced
1½ tablespoons chopped jalapeño chili
2 tablespoons flour
1 tablespoon ground cumin
3 cups chicken broth
½ cup chopped fresh cilantro
½ cup pearl barley
1 pound cooked chicken or turkey, shredded
Salt and freshly ground pepper to taste
1 cup (4 ounces) shredded white Cheddar cheese
1 cup (4 ounces) shredded Monterey jack cheese
1½ cups sliced scallions, including green tops
1 cup diced tomato

Rinse and pick over the chickpeas and beans. Soak them in cold water to cover overnight. Drain.

In a large saucepan, combine the beans with water to cover by several inches. Bring to a boil, reduce heat to a simmer, cover, and cook for 60 to 75 minutes, or until tender. Drain the chickpeas and beans and set aside.

Hollow out the loaves of bread to make "bowls" for the chili. In a large, heavy pot over medium heat, heat the olive oil and sauté the chicken until it loses its color. Add the onion, garlic, and jalapeño. Sauté until the onions are limp, about 4 to 5 minutes. Add the flour and cumin and stir for 2 minutes. Add the chicken broth, chickpeas, beans, and barley. Bring the chili to a boil, then reduce heat, cover, and simmer until the barley is tender, about 45 minutes.

Add the cilantro and shredded chicken and simmer for 15 minutes. Add salt and pepper. Serve the chili in the bread bowls, garnished with cheese, scallions, and tomato.

SMOKED CORNISH HENS WITH LENTIL RAGOUT

When planning your menu, take into consideration the length of time needed to brine, dry, and smoke the hens. You should begin the smoking process at least 3 days in advance of your dinner.

SERVES 6

BRINE

1 gallon water
1 cup kosher salt
¾ cup packed brown sugar
2 tablespoons pickling spice
1 teaspoon garlic powder

6 Rock Cornish game hens, 1 pound each
1 bunch fresh herbs (sage, tarragon, chives, parsley, or thyme)
Lentil Ragout (recipe follows)

TO MAKE THE BRINE: combine all the ingredients in a large stockpot. Bring to a boil and simmer for 10 minutes. Strain. Pour the brine into plastic containers and refrigerate for 2 or 3 hours or until thoroughly chilled. Place the hens in the brine, place a weight on top of the hens to assure that they stay submerged, and refrigerate for 24 hours.

Remove the hens from the brine and rinse them under cold water. Place the hens on a baking sheet and let dry in the refrigerator for 12 to 24 hours. Divide the herbs among the hens, placing them in the birds' cavities. Prepare the smoker following the manufacturer's instructions. Smoke the hens at 250° to 325°F for 3 to 6 hours, or until a thermometer inserted in the thickest portion of the thigh registers 165°F. Let sit for 15 to 20 minutes before serving with the warm lentil ragout. Or, refrigerate both the hens and the ragout and serve chilled.

LENTIL RAGOUT

SERVES 6

1¼ cups French lentils
2 bacon slices, finely chopped
½ cup finely diced onion
¼ cup finely diced celery
¼ cup finely diced carrots
2 garlic cloves, minced
2 tablespoons tomato paste
1 lemon, cut into ½-inch slices
1 bay leaf
4 cups chicken broth
½ teaspoon freshly cracked black pepper
1 teaspoon salt
½ teaspoon caraway seeds
1 teaspoon chopped fresh parsley
1 teaspoon chopped fresh thyme leaves,
    or ¼ teaspoon dried thyme

Rinse and pick over the lentils. In a large, heavy saucepan, sauté the bacon until the fat is rendered. Add the onion, celery, carrot, and garlic, and cook until the onions are translucent. Add the tomato paste and stir. Add the lemon, lentils, bay leaf, broth, pepper, salt, and caraway seeds. Simmer uncovered until the lentils are tender, about 35 to 45 minutes. The lentils should be barely covered with liquid. If there is too much liquid, increase the heat and cook to reduce it. Stir in the parsley and thyme. Taste and adjust the seasonings.

BONELESS FRIED CHICKEN WITH HERBED CREAM SAUCE

Boneless chicken breasts cook quickly and should be carefully watched so they don't overcook.

SERVES 8

4 boneless, skinless whole chicken breasts
2 cups buttermilk
3 egg yolks, beaten
½ teaspoon poultry seasoning
2 cups all-purpose flour
1 teaspoon dried thyme
1 teaspoon dried sage
½ teaspoon dried basil
Lard or vegetable shortening for frying
Herbed Cream Sauce (recipe follows)

Trim the chicken breasts, cut in half, and place them in a shallow baking dish. In a medium bowl, whisk the buttermilk, egg yolks, and poultry seasoning together. Pour this mixture over the chicken. Cover and refrigerate for 4 hours.

In a shallow bowl, stir together the flour, thyme, sage, and basil.

Drain the chicken pieces and dredge them in the seasoned flour. Set aside.

In a large cast-iron skillet over medium-high heat, melt lard or shortening to a depth of ½ inch until the fat shimmers. Add the chicken in a single layer. Cook on the first side for 3 to 5 minutes, or until golden brown. Turn and cook on the other side until firm to the touch and opaque throughout. Drain on paper towels and serve at once with the warm sauce.

HERBED CREAM SAUCE

MAKES 3½ CUPS

2 tablespoons unsalted butter
3 shallots, minced
1 garlic clove, minced
¼ teaspoon paprika
¼ cup dry white wine
Chicken Velouté (see page 61)
1 cup heavy cream
⅓ cup chopped fresh herbs (basil, dill, parsley,
    chervil, tarragon, and/or chives)
Salt and white pepper to taste

In a medium saucepan, melt the butter over medium heat and sauté the shallots, garlic, and paprika until fragrant. Add the wine and cook until reduced by half. Gradually whisk in the velouté and simmer for 5 minutes. Strain the sauce.

Add the cream and herbs. Season with salt and white pepper. Keep warm until serving.

PETTO DI POLLO CON SENAPE, MORTADELLA, E PARMIGIANO
Chicken Breasts with Mustard, Mortadella, and Parmesan
....

SERVES 6

3 boneless, skinless whole chicken breasts, halved
Salt and freshly ground pepper
6 fresh sage leaves, chopped
Flour for dredging
¼ cup olive oil
2 tablespoons Dijon mustard
6 mortadella slices
Parmesan cheese slices

SAUCE

1½ cups chicken broth
2 teaspoons chopped fresh sage
Salt and freshly ground pepper to taste
1½ cups (3 sticks) butter, cut into small pieces

Verdura Mista for serving (see page 32)

Preheat the oven to 350°F. Sprinkle the chicken breasts with the salt, pepper, and sage. Dredge them in the flour.

In a large sauté pan or skillet over high heat, heat the olive oil. Add the chicken (do not crowd the pan) and cook until lightly browned on each side, turning once.

Transfer the chicken to a baking dish and bake for 12 to 15 minutes, or until opaque throughout.

MEANWHILE, TO MAKE THE SAUCE: In a large, heavy saucepan simmer the broth until it is reduced by three quarters, about 10 minutes. Add the sage, salt, and pepper. Gradually whisk in the butter until the sauce is creamy. Set aside and keep warm.

Preheat the broiler. Meanwhile, brush the chicken on top with the mustard. Place a slice of mortadella and cheese on each piece. Place the chicken under the broiler and cook until the cheese is lightly browned, about 2 minutes. Serve at once with the mixed vegetables and sauce.

CHICKEN BAKED IN A SALT CRUST
....

Amazingly enough, this chicken doesn't come out tasting salty. To the contrary, the crust improves the flavor and texture of the bird by sealing in the juices normally lost during roasting.

SERVES 4

4 pounds rock salt
4 egg whites, beaten until frothy
One 2¾-pound chicken
2 tablespoons olive oil
1 lemon, cut in half
4 fresh rosemary sprigs
1 tablespoon freshly ground pepper

Preheat oven to 375°F. In a large bowl, combine rock salt, egg whites, and enough water to make a slushy mixture. In a 10-inch pie pan or similar round dish, spread one fourth of the salt mixture and make a well in the center.

Rub the chicken with the olive oil. Place the lemon halves and 2 rosemary sprigs inside the bird. Rub the outside of the bird with the pepper. Place the remaining rosemary between the breast and skin of bird. Truss the chicken and place it on the salt mixture. Pack the remaining salt mixture evenly around the entire chicken.

Bake the chicken for 50 minutes, or until a thermometer inserted into the thigh through the crust registers 165°F.

Remove the chicken from the oven. With a cleaver or chef's knife, cut a lid one third of the way from the top of the salt crust. Remove the chicken, cut away the string, and carve.

GOAT CHEESE-STUFFED TURKEY BURGERS WITH ROASTED RED PEPPER AND APRICOT RELISH

SERVES 6

1½ pounds ground turkey leg meat
6 tablespoons bread crumbs, toasted (see page 13)
1½ tablespoons fresh lemon juice
1½ teaspoons grated lemon zest
¾ teaspoon chopped fresh thyme
½ to 1 teaspoon salt
Freshly ground pepper to taste
6 tablespoons fresh goat cheese
6 sandwich-size English muffins
Roasted Red Pepper and Apricot Relish (recipe follows)

Light a fire in a charcoal or gas grill.

In a medium bowl, combine the turkey meat, bread crumbs, lemon juice, lemon zest, thyme, salt, and pepper. Blend well. Divide the mixture into 12 equal portions and press them into 4-inch patties.

Top each of 6 patties with 1 tablespoon goat cheese. Place a second patty on top and press down the edges to seal the two together. Place the patties on a baking sheet, cover, and refrigerate for 1 hour.

Brush each burger with oil. Grill on an oiled grill rack over a hot fire for 5 to 6 minutes on each side, or until cooked through. Serve on an English muffin, topped with relish.

ROASTED RED PEPPER AND APRICOT RELISH

MAKES 2 CUPS

3 tablespoons oil
1 cup finely chopped red onion
1 teaspoon minced garlic, finely chopped
1 cup red bell peppers, roasted, peeled, and finely diced (see page 13)
1 cup dried apricots, diced
½ cup chicken broth
3 to 4 teaspoon distilled white vinegar
1 teaspoon honey mustard
2 to 3 drops Tabasco sauce
Freshly ground pepper to taste
1 teaspoon chopped fresh parsley

In a heavy, medium saucepan over medium heat, heat the oil and sauté the onion and garlic for 1 minute. Add the red peppers, apricots, and broth, and simmer for 5 to 10 minutes.

Add the vinegar, mustard, and Tabasco. Cook until most of the liquid has evaporated. Add the pepper.

Serve either at room temperature or chilled. Add the parsley just before serving.

MOROCCAN CHICKEN

SERVES 8

SPICE PASTE

¼ teaspoon cayenne pepper

½ teaspoon paprika

1 teaspoon garlic powder

½ teaspoon ground pepper

½ teaspoon ground cinnamon

½ teaspoon ground cumin

1½ teaspoons fresh lemon juice

1 tablespoon extra-virgin olive oil

8 chicken legs, skinned

2 tablespoons olive oil

1 cup chicken broth

½ cup Kalamata olives, pitted and chopped

6 tomatoes, peeled, seeded, and chopped (see page 22)

5 bell peppers in assorted colors, roasted and chopped
   (see page 13)

1 teaspoon chopped fresh cilantro

1 teaspoon chopped fresh parsley

Salt and freshly ground pepper to taste

Pita bread for serving (see page 48)

TO MAKE THE SPICE PASTE: In a large, shallow bowl, combine all the paste ingredients. Add the chicken legs and turn them to coat them evenly with the paste.

In a large cast-iron skillet or flameproof casserole over medium heat, heat the olive oil, and brown the chicken legs on all sides. Transfer the chicken to a plate. Add the broth to the pan and stir over medium heat to dissolve all the browned bits on the bottom of the pan.

Add the chicken legs and olives to the pan. Bring the broth to a simmer, cover, and braise over low heat until the chicken is fork tender, about 1 hour. Remove the chicken legs from the cooking liquid and let cool until they can be handled.

Pull the meat from the bones and put it in a large bowl. Add the tomatoes, roasted peppers, fresh herbs, and cooking liquid. Toss the mixture well and season generously with salt and pepper. Cover and refrigerate for 1 or 2 hours, or until thoroughly chilled.

To serve, scoop the chicken mixture into fresh pita pockets.

BAKED CATFISH AND DEVILED CRAB
WITH CORN BREAD TOPPING

SERVES 6

SPICE MIXTURE

1½ teaspoons salt
1½ teaspoons garlic powder
1 teaspoon onion powder
1 teaspoon dry mustard
1 teaspoon sweet paprika
1 teaspoon dried basil
½ teaspoon dried thyme
½ teaspoon ground white pepper
¼ teaspoon ground black pepper
¼ teaspoon cayenne pepper
¼ teaspoon ground allspice

4 tablespoons unsalted butter
1 onion, minced
1 celery stalk, minced
1 tablespoon all-purpose flour
1 cup Shrimp Broth (recipe follows)
4 green onions, chopped, including the green
2 egg yolks
8 ounces lump crabmeat, picked over
6 catfish fillets, about 3 ounces each
Salt and freshly ground pepper to taste
½ cup corn bread crumbs
Three-Onion Sauce (recipe follows)
6 fresh parsley sprigs for garnish

Preheat the oven to 375°F. Lightly oil a baking sheet.

In a small bowl, combine all the ingredients for the spice mixture. In a large sauté pan or skillet melt the butter over medium-low heat. Add the onion and celery, and sauté until lightly browned.

Add the spice mixture and cook, stirring, until the mixture begins to brown lightly. Add the flour and cook, stirring occasionally, for about 3 minutes. Stir in the shrimp broth ⅓ cup at a time, stirring after each addition. Simmer until thickened. Add the green onions.

In a small bowl, beat the egg yolks until slightly frothy. Whisk a small amount of the hot sauce into the yolks, then whisk the yolk mixture into the sauce in the pan. Add the crabmeat; stir to heat through, and set aside.

Season the catfish fillets with salt and pepper. Top each fillet with an equal portion of the deviled crabmeat. Bake the fillets on the prepared baking sheet for 8 to 10 minutes, or until the fish is firm and opaque. Increase the oven temperature to broil. Top each fillet with a layer of corn bread crumbs and brown under the broiler.

Serve immediately on a pool of hot sauce, garnished with a parsley sprig.

SHRIMP BROTH

MAKES ABOUT 6 CUPS

2 tablespoons vegetable oil
1 pound shrimp shells
1 onion, coarsely chopped
1 carrot, peeled and coarsely chopped
1 celery stalk, coarsely chopped
2 garlic cloves, chopped
8 cups chicken broth
3 parsley stems
½ teaspoon dried thyme
1 bay leaf
½ teaspoon cracked black peppercorns

In a small stockpot over medium-low heat, heat the oil and sauté the shrimp shells until red and aromatic. Add the onion, carrot, celery, and garlic; sauté until tender and light golden. Add the remaining ingredients, bring to a simmer, and cook, uncovered, for 30 minutes.

Strain the broth through cheesecloth or a very fine-meshed sieve. Let cool and refrigerate for up to 3 days, or freeze for up to 3 months.

THREE-ONION SAUCE

MAKES ABOUT 3 CUPS

2½ tablespoons vegetable oil
3 shallots, minced
½ cup plus 2 tablespoons dry sherry
1 cup Shrimp Broth (recipe precedes)
3 black peppercorns, cracked
2 cups heavy cream
Salt and freshly ground pepper to taste
1 leek, including light green part, halved
*   lengthwise and thinly sliced*
4 green onions, including green part, thinly sliced

In a small saucepan over medium-low heat, heat ½ tablespoon of the oil and sauté one third of the shallots until translucent, about 3 minutes. Add the ½ cup sherry and cook until reduced to a syrup. Add the broth and peppercorns, and cook until reduced to a glaze.

Add the cream and cook until the sauce is thickened and coats the back of a wooden spoon. Season with salt and pepper, and keep warm.

Blanch the leek well in boiling salted water for about 3 minutes, or until softened. Rinse in cold water to halt the cooking process; drain.

In a medium, heavy saucepan over medium-low heat, heat the remaining 2 tablespoons oil and sauté the leeks, remaining shallots, and green onions until softened. Add the 2 tablespoons sherry and cook until almost evaporated. Add the cream mixture, heat through, and season with salt and pepper to taste. Serve hot.

Shredded Turkey with Tomato-Leek Ragout

SERVES 6

½ cup (1 stick) butter
1½ pounds (6 ounces) boneless, skinless turkey breast,
    cut into strips
Salt and freshly ground pepper to taste
⅓ cup kirsch
⅓ cup minced shallot
¾ cup sliced shiitake mushroom caps
1½ tablespoons arrowroot
5 teaspoons Madras curry powder
½ cup dry white wine
½ cup half-and-half
½ cup ketchup
6 tablespoons sour cream
¾ cup julienned mango
Tomato-Leek Ragout (recipe follows)

In a large sauté pan or skillet, melt 4 tablespoons of the butter over medium heat and sear the turkey on both sides for a total of 3 to 4 minutes, or until lightly golden on the outside and opaque throughout. Season with salt, pepper, and kirsch. Transfer to a plate and keep warm.

Add the remaining 4 tablespoons butter to the pan and sauté the shallots for 2 minutes. Add the mushrooms and sauté for 5 minutes. Add the arrowroot and curry powder and sauté for

1 to 2 minutes longer. Add the white wine and half-and-half. Bring to a boil and add the ketchup and turkey.

Remove from the heat and stir in the sour cream. Top each portion with mango. Serve at once with the ragout.

Tomato-Leek Ragout

SERVES 6

¼ cup olive oil
6 garlic cloves, sliced thin
2 cups cubed red onions
3 cups cubed leeks, including green portions
3 tomatoes, peeled, seeded, and chopped (see page 22)
¼ cup ketchup
3 to 4 tablespoons balsamic vinegar
1 teaspoon finely ground espresso roast coffee beans
Salt and freshly ground pepper to taste
¼ cup fresh parsley sprigs

In a large saucepan over medium heat, heat the oil and sauté the garlic until golden. Add the onions and leeks and sauté for 2 to 3 minutes.

Add the tomatoes, ketchup, and vinegar and simmer for 15 minutes. Stir in the espresso and cook until the liquid is evaporated. Season with salt and pepper, then stir in the parsley.

CORNFLAKE-AND-PISTACHIO-CRUSTED SALMON CAKES WITH CUCUMBER-YOGURT RANCH DRESSING

Here is a perfect way to use up any salmon scraps you might have. Smoked salmon can also be used, but will add a new flavor element to the finished cake.

SERVES 4

2 tablespoons corn oil, plus oil for frying
¼ cup minced shallots
2 teaspoons minced garlic
1½ teaspoons ground coriander
1 pound salmon fillet, poached and cut into small dice
¾ cup mayonnaise
1½ teaspoons chopped fresh cilantro
1½ teaspoons chopped fresh tarragon
1½ teaspoons chopped fresh parsley
Old Bay Seasoning to taste
2 teaspoons fresh lemon juice
Salt and freshly ground pepper to taste
½ cup fresh bread crumbs
3 eggs
¼ cup milk
4 cups cornflakes, lightly crushed
¾ cup pistachio nuts, toasted and coarsely ground (see page 13)
Flour for dredging
Cucumber-Yogurt Ranch Dressing (recipe follows)

In a small sauté pan or skillet over medium heat, heat the 2 tablespoons oil and sauté the shallots and garlic until translucent. Add the coriander and sauté until aromatic. Transfer the shallot mixture to a plate or shallow dish and let cool completely.

In a medium bowl, combine the salmon, mayonnaise, fresh herbs, Old Bay, and lemon juice, salt, and pepper. Gradually add just enough bread crumbs to make the mixture adhere well. Scoop the mixture into ¼-cup portions and shape them into cakes.

In a shallow bowl, whisk the eggs and milk together. In a second bowl, stir the cornflakes and nuts together.

Dredge the patties in flour and shake off the excess. Dip each patty into the egg mixture, then the cornflake mixture. Place the patties on a baking sheet.

In a large cast-iron skillet over medium heat, heat about ¼ inch oil until the surface shimmers. Fry the cakes in batches until they are evenly browned on both sides. Drain on paper towels and keep warm in a low oven until all of the cakes are cooked. Serve at once with the dressing.

CUCUMBER-YOGURT RANCH DRESSING

MAKES ABOUT 3½ CUPS

1 cup mayonnaise
2 cups plain yogurt
½ English (hothouse) cucumber, peeled and pureed
2 garlic cloves, minced
3 tablespoons minced shallots, rinsed in cold water
1 tablespoon Dijon mustard
2 tablespoons fresh lemon juice
2 tablespoons white wine vinegar
1 tablespoon chopped fresh dill
1 tablespoon chopped fresh tarragon
1 tablespoon chopped fresh cilantro
1 teaspoon chopped fresh parsley
Salt and freshly ground pepper to taste

In a medium bowl, combine all the ingredients and blend well. Cover and refrigerate for at least 30 minutes. Serve now, or store for up to 2 days. Stir well and check the seasoning before serving.

SEARED SALMON WITH CAULIFLOWER PUREE

SERVES 6

2 heads cauliflower, chopped
½ cup (1 stick) unsalted butter, cut into pieces
⅓ cup heavy cream
Six 5-ounce salmon fillets
Olive oil for brushing
Salt and freshly ground pepper to taste

Steam the cauliflower in a covered pan over boiling water until tender, about 8 to 10 minutes. In a food processor or blender, puree the hot cauliflower. Pour into a bowl and stir in a few pieces of butter and the cream until blended. Set aside and keep warm.

Brush the salmon fillets with the oil and season with salt and pepper. Heat a large nonstick sauté pan or skillet over high heat until smoking and sauté the salmon for 2 to 3 minutes. Turn the fish over and cook another 2 to 3 minutes, or to the desired doneness. Serve at once with the warm puree.

SMOKED SALMON AND POTATO HASH

Brunch menus built around this "uptown" version of home-style hash call for a glass of bubbly or a mimosa.

SERVES 6

2 tablespoons vegetable oil
1 onion, diced
3 Idaho potatoes, peeled and grated
1 carrot, peeled and diced
½ fennel bulb, trimmed, cored, and diced
8 ounces smoked salmon, diced
Salt and white pepper to taste
6 eggs

Preheat the oven to 350°F. In a large sauté pan or skillet over medium-high heat, heat the oil and sauté the onion until translucent, about 4 minutes. Add the potatoes and sauté for about 5 to 6 minutes, or until limp. Add the carrots and fennel and sauté until the potatoes are golden brown. Remove from heat and stir in the salmon. Season with salt and pepper.

Pack the mixture into 6 shallow ramekins or an 8-inch square baking dish. Make a hollow in the center of each portion using a tablespoon. Crack an egg into each hollow.

Bake for about 8 minutes, or until the eggs are opaque.

TAGINE OF HALIBUT WITH PRESERVED LEMONS AND CAPERBERRIES

....

Tagine is the name of a traditional Moroccan cooking vessel, as well as the stewlike dishes cooked in it. An ordinary heavy casserole dish may be used to cook this dish.

SERVES 6

HERB MIXTURE

⅔ cup coarsely chopped fresh flat-leaf parsley
¼ cup coarsely chopped fresh cilantro
1 tablespoon minced garlic
⅓ cup virgin olive oil
1 teaspoon pepper
Sea salt to taste
Juice of 1 lemon
1 tablespoon hot paprika
1 pinch cayenne pepper
1 teaspoon ground cumin

Six 6-ounce halibut steaks, skinned
½ teaspoon crushed saffron threads
½ cup boiling water
1 cup very thinly sliced onion
½ cup very thinly sliced fennel
2 carrots, peeled and sliced
2 celery stalks, very thinly sliced
3 cups plum tomatoes, halved, seeded, and chopped
1 tablespoon minced garlic
½ cup caperberries (see Chef's Tip)
1 Preserved Lemon, rinsed and slivered (recipe follows)
Sea salt and freshly ground pepper to taste
¼ cup virgin olive oil

Preheat the oven to 425°F. In a bowl, combine all the ingredients for the herb mixture. Place the fish in a shallow baking dish and rub mixture on all sides of the fish. Cover and refrigerate for at least 2 hours.

In a small bowl, combine the saffron and boiling water. Let sit for 30 minutes.

Combine the vegetables with the garlic, caperberries, preserved lemon, salt, and pepper; toss well. Place the vegetable mixture in the bottom of a large ovenproof casserole. Drizzle the vegetable bed with the saffron-infused water and olive oil. Place the fish on top of the vegetable bed.

Cover the casserole with a lid or aluminum foil and bake for 25 to 30 minutes, or until the fish is opaque throughout.

Serve the fish on a bed of the vegetables, sprinkled with a little of the cooking liquid.

CHEF'S TIP: Caperberries, which are larger than standard capers, are available from specialty foods or Mediterranean markets.

PRESERVED LEMONS

Lemons preserved in salt lose their sharpness and gain a mellow flavor. They keep well, almost indefinitely, so make a double batch to use in other dishes.

MAKES 4 CUPS

8 organic lemons, scrubbed
2 cups water
1 cup kosher salt
Fresh lemon juice, if needed

Sterilize a 1-quart canning jar by immersing it in boiling water for 10 minutes Set aside, using tongs. Cut the lemons in quarters from the flower tip to within ½ inch of the stem end. Tightly pack the lemons into the jar.

In a medium saucepan, bring the water to a boil and stir in the salt until dissolved. Fill the jar completely with the salt water and cover tightly. Let sit at room temperature for 24 hours. If the water is not up to the brim of the jar, add lemon juice to make up the difference. Refrigerate for 2 weeks before using.

BAKED SCROD, GARDEN STYLE

Scrod, a term familiar throughout the Boston area, refers to baby cod, haddock, or pollock weighing under 2½ pounds. Any firm-fleshed white fish may be used in this recipe.

SERVES 6

4 tablespoons unsalted butter, melted
3 tomatoes, halved lengthwise and cut
  into ¼-inch-thick crosswise slices
Six 8-ounce scrod fillets
Salt and freshly ground pepper to taste
3 cups shredded zucchini
3 tablespoons grated Parmesan cheese
1 cup prepared seasoned bread crumbs
¼ cup chopped fresh herbs: parsley, chives, dill
⅓ cup dry white wine

Preheat the oven to 375°F. Brush individual oval gratin dishes or a large oval or rectangular baking dish with some of the butter.

Brush the tomato slices with a little butter also. You should have about 2 tablespoons of butter remaining. Season the fish and tomatoes lightly with salt and pepper.

Toss the zucchini, Parmesan cheese, 3 tablespoons of the bread crumbs, and the fresh herbs together in a dish with the remaining butter. Season with salt and pepper.

Make a nest of zucchini in the center of each baking dish or make 6 nests in the large dish. Place the buttered fish in the center of each nest. Tuck the tomato slices around the nest, with the straight side of the slices toward the fish.

Place the remaining bread crumbs on top of the fish fillet. Pat the bread crumbs down to form a crust when the fish is cooked. Sprinkle the wine over the vegetables. Bake for 20 to 25 minutes, or until the fish is opaque throughout. Increase the oven temperature to broil. Place the fish under the broiler briefly to brown the bread crumbs.

CHEF'S TIP: Replace each portion of scrod with 2 clams, 2 ounces flounder fillet, 2 ounces salmon fillet, 2 ounces bay scallops, and 2 peeled jumbo shrimp.

SMOKED TROUT WITH APPLE-HORSERADISH CREAM

If you prefer, use 6 pan-dressed trout in this recipe. Leave the head, tail, and skin on during the smoking process for added flavor and to keep the flesh from drying out.

SERVES 6

12 trout fillets, skin on
1 cup kosher salt
½ cup sugar
1 tablespoon garlic powder
1 teaspoon onion powder
1 teaspoon black pepper, freshly ground
Grated zest of 2 lemons
2 handfuls mixed baby greens
Lemon Vinaigrette (recipe follows)
Apple-Horseradish Cream (recipe follows)
2 Granny Smith apples, cored, peeled, and sliced thin

Scrape the skin of each fillet lightly with the back side of a knife to remove the scales. Lay the trout on a baking sheet skin-side down. Combine the salt, sugar, garlic, onion powder, pepper, and lemon zest. Cover the belly and tail sections of the trout with a ⅛-inch layer of the salt mixture and cover the thicker sections with a ¼-inch layer. Let sit for 30 minutes. Rinse the trout in cold water and place them on a wire rack. Let dry, uncovered, in the refrigerator, for 6 to 12 hours.

Prepare a smoker according to the manufacturer's instructions. Place the trout skin-side down in the smoker and let it smoke for 30 to 60 minutes at 225° to 250°F. Let cool.

Toss the greens with the vinaigrette. Serve the trout with the greens, sliced apples, and apple-horseradish sauce.

LEMON VINAIGRETTE

MAKES ABOUT ¾ CUP

¼ cup fresh lemon juice
½ cup vegetable oil
¼ cup sugar
Salt and white pepper to taste

Combine all the ingredients in a small bowl and whisk thoroughly.

APPLE-HORSERADISH CREAM

MAKES ¾ CUP

¼ cup heavy cream
¼ cup sour cream
¼ cup grated peeled Granny Smith apple
1½ tablespoons prepared horseradish
¼ teaspoon salt

In a deep bowl, beat the cream until stiff peaks form. Fold in the sour cream, apple, horseradish, and salt.

FIRECRACKER SHRIMP

SERVES 6

1 pound white Gulf shrimp
3 tablespoons extra-virgin olive oil
2 teaspoons grated lemon zest
¼ teaspoon cayenne pepper
2 teaspoons minced fresh thyme
2 tablespoons minced flat-leaf parsley
5 ounces pancetta, thinly sliced
Juice of 1 lemon

Light a fire in a charcoal or gas grill. Shell the shrimp, leaving the tail on, and devein. In a medium bowl, combine the olive oil, lemon zest, cayenne, thyme, and all but 2 teaspoons of the parsley. Add the shrimp, stir to coat, and marinate for 2 hours. Wrap each shrimp in a slice of pancetta, overlapping the pancetta slightly with each turn to completely cover the shrimp. Thread the shrimp on skewers.

Cook the shrimp over a hot fire for 2 minutes on each side, or until the pancetta begins to color and the shrimp are pink and opaque throughout.

Remove the shrimp from the skewers. Toss with the lemon juice and reserved parsley. Serve at once.

SAUTÉED SOFT-SHELL CRABS

The trick here is not to crowd the crabs in the pan. If necessary, sauté only 1 or 2 at a time. The results will be worth the extra effort.

SERVES 6

12 soft-shell crabs
Kosher salt and freshly ground pepper to taste
1½ cups bread flour
1 cup (2 sticks) unsalted butter at room temperature
Juice of 1 lemon
1 cup chopped fresh parsley, chervil, or tarragon

Season the crabs on both sides with salt and pepper. Dredge in the flour.

In a large sauté pan or skillet, melt ½ cup of the butter. Place the crabs bottom-side down in the pan. Cook the crabs slowly, allowing the butter to brown. When the edges of the crabs are lightly browned, carefully turn them and cook on the second side until crisp and brown. Transfer to a platter.

Put the remaining butter and the lemon juice in the pan. Shake pan so that the butter and lemon juice emulsify with the browned butter in the pan. Stir to scrape up the browned bits from the bottom, add the herbs, and pour the butter mixture over the crabs.

MOROCCAN SPICED LAMB SHANKS

No other dish truly embodies the essence of the Mediterranean as well as this one.

SERVES 6

SPICE MIXTURE

1 teaspoon ground coriander
½ teaspoon ground green cardamom
½ teaspoon ground cumin
½ teaspoon ground allspice
3 teaspoons ground turmeric
2 teaspoons ground cinnamon
½ teaspoon red pepper flakes

6 whole lamb shanks
Salt and freshly ground pepper to taste
¼ cup olive oil
1 cup diced onions
1 celery stalk, cut into small dice
2 to 3 garlic cloves, crushed
2 tomatoes, seeded and diced
1 cup dry red wine
1 cup diced peeled apple
4 cups chicken broth
4 tablespoons unsalted butter
2 cups apple wedges
Couscous for serving
¼ cup sliced almonds, toasted (see page 13)
¼ cup harissa (see page 20)

Preheat the oven to 325°F. Combine all the ingredients for the spice mixture and mix thoroughly. Season shanks with the salt, pepper, and spice mixture.

In a large Dutch oven or ovenproof casserole over medium heat, heat the oil. Add the shanks and brown all over. Pour off the excess oil. Add the onions and celery and cook until brown, about 5 minutes. Add garlic and tomatoes and cook for 2 to 3 minutes. Pour in the wine. Stir with wooden spoon to scrape up all the browned bits on the bottom of the casserole. Add the diced apple and chicken broth. Bring to a simmer, cover and braise in the oven until tender, about 1½ hours. Remove the shanks and keep warm.

Puree the braising liquid and vegetables. If too thick, add a little more broth. If too thin, cook over medium heat to reduce. Taste and adjust the seasonings. Return the shanks to the pot.

In a medium sauté pan or skillet, melt the butter over medium heat and sauté the apple wedges until light golden in color.

Serve the shanks and sauce over couscous, garnished with the apple wedges and toasted almonds. Serve the harissa alongside.

GRILLED HERB-MARINATED STEAK FAJITAS

This "roll your own" meal is a favorite for easy entertaining. Put garnishes and condiments such as fresh salsa, lettuce, shredded cheese, or diced onion in decorative bowls and let your guests choose their own.

SERVES 6

2 pounds skirt steaks
¼ cup fresh lime juice (about 2 limes)
1 jalapeño chili, coarsely chopped
2 garlic cloves, minced
½ teaspoon fresh-cracked black pepper
1 cup chopped cilantro leaves and stems
2 tablespoons cumin seeds, toasted (see page 14)
¼ cup chopped fresh oregano, or 1 tablespoon dried oregano
1 teaspoon salt
Twelve 10-inch flour tortillas

Trim all visible fat from the skirt steaks and cut them against the grain into 6-inch-long pieces.

In a small bowl, combine the lime juice, jalapeño, garlic, pepper, cilantro, cumin, oregano, and salt. In a 1-gallon freezer bag, layer the steak pieces with 1 tablespoon of herb mixture between each piece. Squeeze the excess air out of the bag and seal it. Marinate the steaks for 2 to 3 hours in the refrigerator, turning the bag periodically so that the meat is marinated evenly.

Light a fire in a charcoal or gas grill. Twenty minutes before grilling, remove the steaks from the bag and scrape off the excess herb mixture. Cover and let sit at room temperature.

Grill the steaks over a hot fire for 2 to 3 minutes on each side for medium rare. Grill the tortillas for 15 seconds on each side. Do not allow them to crisp. Place them in a basket lined with a warm towel and serve at once with the beef.

BLACKENED PRIME RIB

The blackening spices take this all-time American favorite to a new realm.

SERVES 6

BLACKENING SPICES

2 teaspoons salt
2 teaspoons sweet paprika
2 teaspoons white pepper
1 teaspoon onion powder
1 teaspoon garlic powder
1 teaspoon cayenne pepper
2 teaspoons black pepper
1 teaspoon dried thyme
1 teaspoon dried basil
½ teaspoon dry mustard

6 boneless rib steaks, trimmed of fat
1 cup (2 sticks) unsalted butter, melted

Combine all the ingredients for the spice mixture and stir to blend.

Brush the steaks generously with the melted butter. Dredge them evenly in the blackening mixture. Heat a large cast-iron skillet over high heat until it is smoking. Place the steaks in the pan without crowding them. Cook them on the first side until the blood rises to the surface, about 2 minutes. Turn the steaks and blacken them on the second side, about 2 minutes for medium rare.

Place the steaks on heated plates, top each with a little melted butter, and serve.

OSSO BUCO ALLA MILANESE
Braised Veal Shanks, Milan Style

A classic accompaniment for this dish is a rich, creamy risotto.

SERVES 6

BATTUTO

½ cup (1 stick) butter
½ cup olive oil
1 cup finely chopped onion
¾ cup finely chopped carrot
¾ cup finely chopped celery

6 veal shanks, cut into 2-inch-thick slices
Salt and freshly ground pepper to taste
Flour for dredging
¼ cup olive oil
1 cup dry white wine
2 cups chicken broth
1 cup finely chopped fresh tomatoes or canned crushed tomatoes
½ teaspoon minced fresh thyme
3 bay leaves
1 tablespoon chopped fresh flat-leaf parsley

GREMOLATA

1 teaspoon grated lemon zest
¼ teaspoon minced garlic
1 tablespoon chopped fresh flat-leaf parsley

Preheat the oven to 350°F.

TO MAKE THE BATTUTO: In a large Dutch oven or heavy flameproof casserole over high heat, melt the butter with the olive oil. Add the onions, carrots, and celery, and cook until tender, about 6 to 8 minutes. Spread the battuto into an even layer in the bottom of the pan.

Season the shanks with salt and pepper and dredge them in flour. In a large sauté pan or skillet over high heat, heat the oil and brown the veal pieces on all sides. Transfer the shanks to the pan and put them on top of the battuto.

Add the wine to the browning pan and stir over medium heat to scrape up all the browned bits from the bottom of the pan. Pour this mixture over the shanks.

Add enough of the broth to cover the shanks by three quarters. Add the tomatoes, thyme, bay leaves, and parsley. Bring the broth to a simmer, cover the casserole, and braise in the oven for 2 hours, or until the veal is fork tender.

Combine all the ingredients for the gremolata. Serve the osso buco with the gremolata sprinkled over it.

FILLETTO DI BUE ALLA CONTADINA
Stuffed Tournedos of Beef

SERVES 6

6 beef tenderloin steaks, about 6 ounces each, trimmed
2 cups beef broth
6 tablespoons olive oil
1 tablespoon minced onion
1 garlic clove, minced
1 tablespoon capers, drained
6 black olives, pitted and chopped
6 anchovy fillets
Salt and freshly ground pepper to taste
1 cup chopped tomatoes
1 teaspoon fresh parsley
¾ cup dry red wine

In a heavy, medium saucepan, simmer the broth over medium-low heat until reduced to 1 cup. In a large sauté pan or skillet over medium heat, heat 3 tablespoons of the oil and sauté the onion until tender but not browned. Add the garlic, capers, olives, and anchovies. Season with salt and pepper. Refrigerate for at least 1 hour, or until chilled.

Using the tip of a paring or boning knife, cut a small opening in each of the steaks. Without enlarging the opening, wiggle the knife tip to create a pocket. Fill the pockets in the steak with the stuffing. Season the steaks with salt and pepper to taste. In a large sauté pan or skillet, heat the remaining 3 tablespoons oil and sauté the steaks on one side for 3 minutes, or until lightly browned. Turn and cook on the second side for 2 minutes for medium rare.

Pour off the fat in the pan. Add the reduced broth and tomatoes. Increase heat and bring to a boil and add the parsley. Add the wine and cook over medium heat, stirring to scrape up the browned bits from the bottom of the pan. Taste and adjust the seasonings. Serve on heated plates, with the sauce spooned over.

GRILLED ASIAN PORK CHOPS

Combining fruit with pork is a time-honored tradition. The sweet-tart flavor of apricots acts as a perfect foil to the spicy pork chops in this dish.

SERVES 6

MARINADE
2 garlic cloves
½ teaspoon aniseed
½ teaspoon salt
¼ cup soy sauce
2 tablespoon Asian (dark) sesame oil

6 pork chops
1 cup chopped bottled pimientos, drained
6 fresh apricots, halved and pitted
¼ cup ketchup
Grated zest of 1 lemon
2 garlic cloves, crushed
¾ cup chicken broth
Salt to taste
Thai Jasmine Rice (see page 43)

TO MAKE THE MARINADE: In a large mortar, crush the garlic cloves, aniseed, and salt together to make a paste. Stir in the soy sauce and sesame oil. Put the chops in a shallow baking dish. Rub the pork chops with the marinade. Cover and refrigerate for 2 to 3 hours.

Light a fire in a charcoal or gas grill. Remove the pork chops from the marinade.

In a small saucepan, combine the pimientos, apricots, ketchup, lemon zest, garlic, and chicken broth, and simmer for 30 minutes. Puree and strain through a fine-meshed sieve. The consistency should be that of syrup. Adjust it if necessary by reducing it further or adding more broth. Season with salt. Set aside and keep warm.

Grill the chops over a medium-hot fire for 5 minutes on each side. Serve with the rice and the sauce on the side.

DESSERTS

L ife is uncertain: Eat dessert first."
From the elegance of a classic Linzer-
torte to updated favorites like grilled
pound cake with grilled bananas, you can find a
dessert for almost any occasion in this chapter. If
you are looking for old-time favorites, try warm
lemon pudding cakes, fresh fruit cobbler or skillet
cake, or a batch of apple-spice muffins with a
streusel topping.

Many of these desserts feature fresh fruits, for a
light ending to a meal. But for those times when
only chocolate will do, we have selected several
special recipes. Some of these, like our own varia-
tion on chocolate cream slices (rigó jansci), feature
that all time favorite flavor pairing—chocolate and
espresso.

CAPPUCCINO SMOOTHIES

SERVES 6 TO 8

2 cups cold brewed espresso or double-strength coffee
1 pint coffee ice cream
6 cups ice
1½ cups milk
Whipped cream as needed
Ground cinnamon as needed

In a blender, blend the espresso, ice cream, ice, and milk until smooth. Divide among six to eight stemmed glasses. Top each with a dollop of whipped cream and a sprinkle of cinnamon. Serve with a straw.

FOR A MOCHA CAPPUCCINO: Substitute chocolate sorbet for the ice cream and chocolate milk for the regular milk. Sprinkle cocoa or chocolate shavings instead of cinnamon.

COLD STRAWBERRY SOUP

Be sure to make this soup when strawberries are at the height of their season in your area.

SERVES 6

4 cups strawberries
⅓ cup sugar
¼ cup strawberry liqueur
3 cups heavy cream
3 cups apple juice
1 teaspoon fresh lemon juice
½ cup honey

Reserve 1 large berry for garnish. In a large nonreactive bowl, combine the remaining strawberries, the sugar, and liqueur and refrigerate for 2 to 24 hours. Puree the berries.

Add all the remaining ingredients to the berries. Mix well, cover, and refrigerate for at least 2 or 3 hours.

Serve the soup very cold in chilled cups. Cut the reserved berry into paper-thin slices. Garnish each serving with a slice of strawberry.

TROPICAL FRUIT SMOOTHIES

For a truly tropical treat, serve these fruit drinks in a tall hurricane glass and garnish each with a pineapple spear and a sprinkle of toasted coconut.

SERVES 6

1 cup diced mango
1 cup diced papaya
2 cups diced pineapple
1 kiwi, peeled and diced
1½ cups fresh orange juice
½ cup coconut milk
Sugar or honey as needed
¼ teaspoon vanilla extract
¾ cup plain nonfat yogurt (optional)
1 cup ice

GARNISH
8 pineapple spears
¼ cup unsweetened coconut, toasted (see note)

In a blender, combine all the fruits and half of the orange juice. Puree until quite smooth. With the machine running, add the remaining ingredients and blend until smooth and thick.

Serve garnished with a pineapple spear and toasted coconut. TO TOAST COCONUT: Swirl the grated coconut in a dry sauté pan over medium-high heat for 2 to 3 minutes, or until golden brown. Immediately pour the toasted coconut into a cool bowl or plate to prevent scorching.

ESPRESSO SMOOTHIES

Double strength coffee can be used if espresso is not available.

SERVES 6

3 cups cold brewed espresso, or double-strength coffee
6 cups ice
6 rock sugar swizzle sticks, or sugar as needed
6 lemon wedges

In a blender, blend the espresso and ice until smooth. Add a swizzle stick to each glass. If using sugar, rub the rim of each glass with a lemon wedge, then dip it in sugar. Divide the mixture among 6 stemmed glasses and serve with lemon wedges and straws.

GRILLED PEPPERED PINEAPPLE WITH TEQUILA AND ORANGE SAUCE

Surprise your family and friends with this sweet-hot grilled dessert at your next barbecue.

SERVES 6

1 large pineapple
1½ teaspoons green peppercorns, minced
¼ cup honey, preferably buckwheat
1½ cups orange juice
4 ounces silver tequila
1 pint vanilla ice cream

Light a fire in a charcoal or gas grill. Using a large kitchen knife, cut off the top and bottom of the pineapple. Cut off the skin down to the flesh. Cut the pineapple into ½- to ¾-inch cross-wise slices. Remove the core with a round cutter. Rub both sides of the pineapple slices with the peppercorns.

In a small, heavy saucepan, combine the honey, orange juice, and tequila. Cook over medium heat until reduced by three fourths. The sauce will appear slightly thick. Set aside and keep warm.

Grill the pineapple slices on a well-oiled grill over a hot fire until both sides are well browned. Divide among 6 dessert plates. Drizzle each serving with 1 tablespoon of sauce and top with vanilla ice cream. Serve immediately.

GRANOLA, YOGURT, AND FRESH FRUIT PARFAITS

Serve these for breakfast, or for an afternoon pick-me-up.

SERVES 6

3 cups granola
3 cups mixed fresh berries
3 cups plain or flavored yogurt
6 tablespoons heavy cream, lightly whipped
6 fresh mint sprigs

Alternate 3 or 4 layers each of granola, fruit, and yogurt in each of 6 parfait or pilsner glasses. Top each with a dollop of whipped cream and a mint sprig.

CHEF'S TIP: Any fresh ripe fruits can be used, depending on what is available. If the fruits are large, cut them into ½-inch dice. If using citrus fruits, grate some of the zest and add it to the whipped cream.

APPLE, PRUNE, AND ARMAGNAC BEGGARS PURSES

In Greek, *phyllo* means "leaf." This tissue thin pastry dough can be tricky to work with at first, but once you get the hang of it, phyllo can be used to make an endless variety of sweet and savory items.

SERVES 6

12 prunes, pitted
¾ cup Armagnac or brandy
12 Granny Smith apples, peeled, cored and cut into 1-inch dice
1 teaspoon freshly grated nutmeg, plus more for dusting
½ cup granulated sugar
6 tablespoons butter, melted
9 phyllo dough sheets
Powdered sugar for dusting
1 pint vanilla ice cream

In a small saucepan, bring the prunes and Armagnac or brandy to a simmer. Remove from heat, cover, and let sit.

Preheat the oven to 350° F. In a large bowl, combine the apples, 1 teaspoon nutmeg, sugar, and 2 tablespoons of the melted butter. Drain the prunes, cut them into ½-inch pieces, and stir them into the apple mixture.

Cut the phyllo sheets into quarters. Place 6 phyllo squares on a work surface. Brush the sheets lightly with some of the remaining melted butter. Top each with a second square and brush with butter. Repeat this process until you have 5 layers.

Divide the filling equally among the phyllo stacks. Top each with a final square. Fold them into pouches by pulling up the edges and twisting the top closed.

Dust the tops with nutmeg. Bake for 35 minutes, or until the phyllo is golden brown. Sift powdered sugar over the purses and serve them immediately with ice cream.

GRILLED POUND CAKE WITH GRILLED BANANAS AND RED WINE SAUCE

The red wine sauce can be prepared in advance and the entire dessert assembled in a matter of minutes, letting you get back to more important things.

SERVES 6

RED WINE SAUCE

1¼ cups dry red wine
¼ cup sugar
¼ stick cinnamon
1 clove
½ to 1 teaspoon arrowroot
Juice of 1 orange

6 slices pound cake, ½ inch thick
½ cup (1 stick) butter, melted
3 firm bananas, peeled and cut in half lengthwise
Vanilla ice cream for serving (optional)

Light a fire in a charcoal or gas grill.

TO MAKE THE SAUCE: In a small, heavy saucepan, combine the red wine, sugar, cinnamon, and clove. Bring to a boil. Combine the arrowroot and orange juice and stir into the red wine mixture. Continue to cook over medium heat until thickened. Remove from heat and let cool to room temperature.

Brush the pound cake on both sides with butter and grill for 1 to 2 minutes on each side, or until lightly colored. Brush the bananas with butter and grill them for about 30 seconds per side, or until lightly colored.

Place each slice of pound cake on a dessert plate. Top with a banana and vanilla ice cream and drizzle with the red wine sauce.

TIRAMISÙ

....

Tiramisù means "pick-me-up," and a little jolt of espresso does give a lift to this popular Italian dessert.

SERVES 6

1 egg
6 egg yolks
1½ cups granulated sugar
1 teaspoon vanilla extract
26 ounces mascarpone cheese at room temperature
3 egg whites
1 cup cold brewed espresso
½ cup Kahlúa
2 packages ladyfingers
¼ cup unsweetened cocoa powder
2 tablespoons powdered sugar

In a double boiler over barely simmering water, whisk the egg, egg yolks, 1 cup of the sugar, and the vanilla together for about 3 minutes, or until the volume nearly doubles and the mixture becomes a light lemon yellow.

Remove from heat and beat the egg mixture on high speed until it has cooled to room temperature. Add the mascarpone and blend on low speed until very smooth. Scrape the sides and bottom of the bowl to blend evenly.

In a large bowl, beat the egg whites with the remaining ½ cup sugar until stiff, glossy peaks form. Fold the beaten egg whites into the mascarpone mixture in thirds. Refrigerate until needed.

Combine the espresso and Kahlúa to make a syrup. Place a layer of ladyfingers in a 6-cup bowl. Moisten the ladyfingers well with the syrup and dust evenly with the cocoa powder. Top with a 1-inch thick layer of the mascarpone filling. Repeat layering in this sequence until all the components are used, ending with a layer of filling.

Dust the entire surface of the cake with cocoa power and powdered sugar. Refrigerate for at least 2 hours or until thoroughly chilled before serving.

PEAR NAPOLEONS
WITH RASPBERRY PUREE

This version of napoleons is significantly lighter than the classic pastry-cream filled version.

SERVES 10

HONEY CRISPS

2 tablespoons butter at room temperature
3 tablespoons powdered sugar
⅓ cup honey
¼ cup flour
1 egg white

FILLING

2 cups sweet white wine
½ vanilla bean, halved lengthwise
4 Bartlett pears, peeled and cored
1 cup ricotta cheese
2 tablespoons honey
Raspberry Puree (recipe follows)
Powdered sugar for dusting

Preheat the oven to 350°F. Line a baking sheet with parchment paper or grease it.

TO MAKE THE HONEY CRISPS: In a medium bowl, cream the butter and powdered sugar together. Add the honey and blend thoroughly. Add the flour and stir until the mixture is smooth. Add the egg white and mix, scraping the bottom and sides of the bowl, until the batter is very smooth.

Spread about 1 tablespoon of the batter on the prepared sheet to make a cookie about 3 inches in diameter. Leave 1 inch between the cookies. Bake for 3 to 4 minutes, or until the edges just begin to brown. Using a flexible metal spatula, remove the honey crisps from the baking sheet and let cool on a wire rack.

TO MAKE THE FILLING: In a large saucepan, combine the wine and the vanilla bean. Bring to a simmer and add the pears. Poach until the pears are tender but still hold their shape. Let cool in the liquid. Drain and slice the pears.

In a small bowl, mix the ricotta cheese and honey until thoroughly blended. Pool raspberry sauce on each plate. Spread the ricotta mixture on each of 6 crisps. Top with pear slices and a second crisp. Dust the tops with powdered sugar. Set each napoleon on a pool of sauce and serve at once.

RASPBERRY PUREE

MAKES ¾ CUP

¼ cup sugar
¼ cup burgundy wine
2½ cups fresh raspberries, pureed and strained

In a large saucepan, combine all the ingredients. Bring to a simmer and cook for 3 minutes. Strain through a fine-meshed sieve. Cover and refrigerate until needed.

ALMOND CUSTARD WITH POACHED DRIED FRUIT

SERVES 6

1½ cups milk
¾ cup half-and-half
1⅔ cups sugar
½-inch piece vanilla bean
½ teaspoon almond extract
3 eggs
2 egg yolks
¼ cup plus 3 tablespoons water
¼ teaspoon fresh lemon juice
Poached Dried Fruit (recipe follows)

In a heavy, medium saucepan, combine the milk, half-and-half, and ⅔ cup of the sugar. Split the vanilla bean in half and scrape out the seeds. Add the seeds and the pod to the milk mixture. Bring to a simmer, stirring until the sugar dissolves. Remove the pan from heat, and add the almond extract. Let cool to lukewarm

In a large bowl, whisk the eggs and egg yolks together. Whisk in half of the warm milk mixture. Whisk in the remaining milk mixture. Cover and refrigerate for at least 2 to 3 hours.

Preheat the oven to 350° F. In a heavy, small saucepan, heat the remaining 1 cup of sugar in a saucepan with the ¼ cup water and the lemon juice over low heat until the sugar is dissolved. Increase heat and boil without stirring until the mixture turns a deep brown, swirling the pan and occasionally brushing down the sides with a wet pastry brush to dissolve any crystals clinging to the sides of the pan. Add the 3 tablespoons water to the caramel and stir over low heat until any hard bits are dissolved. Immediately divide the caramel evenly among 6 custard cups. Quickly swirl

the cups to coat them with the caramel part way up the sides of the cup.

Pour the custard mixture into the prepared cups and place them in a baking dish. Add enough hot water to come halfway up the sides of the cups. Cover the entire container tightly with aluminum foil.

Place the pan in the oven and bake for about 40 minutes, or until the center of the custard moves only slightly. Remove the custards from the water bath. Refrigerate for at least 2 hours before serving.

To serve, run a sharp knife around the edges of each cup. Turn each custard out onto a chilled plate. Garnish with the poached fruit.

POACHED DRIED FRUIT

MAKES 2 CUPS

¼ cup sugar
1½ cups water
1-inch vanilla bean, split in half lengthwise
Juice of 1 lemon
½ cup dried apricots
¼ cup dried currants
½ cup dried cherries or strawberries
½ cup golden raisins

In a medium saucepan, combine the sugar, water, and vanilla bean and lemon juice. Bring to a boil, and pour over the dried fruit. Let the fruit set for 20 to 30 minutes, or until the fruit is plump and tender. Serve at once, or cover and store in the refrigerator for up to 3 days. Store the fruit in the syrup until you are ready to serve it. If refrigerated, let sit at room temperature for 30 minutes before serving. To serve, remove the fruit from the syrup with a slotted spoon.

CHOCOLATE MOUSSE WITH FRESH RASPBERRIES

Raspberry and chocolate are a classic culinary combination. Why deny yourself?

SERVES 6

3¾ cups heavy cream
¼ cup dark rum (optional)
1 tablespoon sugar
½ teaspoon vanilla extract
8 ounces semisweet chocolate, chopped
1 cup fresh raspberries
Chocolate curls for garnish

In a deep bowl, lightly whip 3 cups of the cream and flavor it with the rum, if you like. In another deep bowl, whip the remaining ¾ cup cream with the sugar and vanilla until stiff peaks form.

Melt the chocolate in a double boiler over barely simmering water. Add 1 cup of the lightly whipped cream to the chocolate and whisk to combine the two. Stir the chocolate mixture gently until it becomes the same consistency as the remaining lightly whipped cream.

Fold the chocolate mixture into the remaining lightly whipped cream until they are a smooth, homogenous mixture. (Do not overmix.)

Place a few raspberries at the bottom of each of six 6-ounce wineglasses. Pipe or spoon the chocolate mousse into each glass to within 1 inch of the top. Divide the remaining raspberries evenly and place on top of the mousse in each glass.

Using a medium star tip, pipe a rosette of the stiffly whipped cream on top of the berries. Refrigerate the mousse for at least 3 hours. Garnish with chocolate curls just before serving.

PANNA COTTA
Cooked Cream

MAKES 6 SERVINGS

1 package plain gelatin
¼ cup cold water
2½ cups heavy cream
1 cup sugar
2⅓ cups buttermilk
¼ teaspoon salt
2 cups sliced fresh fruit or berries

In a small bowl, sprinkle the gelatin over the cold water. Let sit for 3 minutes.

Meanwhile, in a large saucepan, heat the cream and sugar over low heat until the sugar dissolves. Remove from heat and stir the softened gelatin into the warm cream. Stir in the buttermilk and salt. Fill individual glass bowls or one large glass bowl with the fruit. Ladle the cream mixture over the fruit. Cover and refrigerate for at least 3 hours or up to 24 hours in the refrigerator before serving.

FLORENTINERS

....

MAKES 4 DOZEN 1½-INCH SQUARES

DOUGH

1 cup (2 sticks) unsalted butter at room temperature
½ cup sugar
1 egg
3⅔ cups cake flour, sifted
½ teaspoon salt

TOPPING

½ cup honey
¾ cup (1½ sticks) unsalted butter
1¼ cups sugar
1½ cups heavy cream
2 cups (8 ounces) sliced raw almonds
¾ cups dried cherries, finely chopped
⅓ cup cake flour

TO MAKE THE DOUGH: In a large bowl, cream the butter and sugar together until smooth and fluffy. Add the egg, mixing well and scraping down the sides of the bowl as necessary. Add the flour and salt; mix until just incorporated. Transfer the dough to a baking sheet. Press into a rectangle about 1 inch thick. Refrigerate for 20 minutes.

Preheat the oven to 375°F.

On a lightly floured board, roll the dough out into a 15-by-10-inch rectangle. Transfer it to a jelly roll pan and press it to fit. Prick the dough all over with a fork. Bake for 12 minutes, or until slightly brown around the edges. Remove from the oven, leaving the oven on. Let cool.

TO MAKE THE TOPPING: In a large, heavy saucepan, bring the honey, butter, sugar, and heavy cream to a boil. Cook until a candy thermometer registers 240°F, or until a small amount dropped in a glass of cold water forms a soft, malleable ball. Remove from heat and stir in the sliced almonds, cherries, and cake flour. Pour the mixture over the dough and spread evenly, using a wet rubber spatula.

Bake until golden brown, about 15 minutes. Let cool. Cut into 1½-inch squares to serve.

APPLE-SPICE MUFFINS

This recipe produces a dense, moist muffin with the aroma and flavor of a freshly baked apple pie.

MAKES 24 MUFFINS

1 cup raisins
1½ cups diced Granny Smith apples
¼ cup dark rum, heated
3 cups all-purpose flour
4 teaspoons baking powder
1 tablespoon ground cinnamon
1 teaspoon ground nutmeg
¾ teaspoon ground cloves
1⅓ cups milk
2 teaspoons vanilla extract
1⅓ cups sugar
½ cup (1 stick) plus 1 tablespoon unsalted butter
    at room temperature
5 tablespoons vegetable shortening
1 teaspoon salt
3 large eggs
Streusel Topping (recipe follows)

Preheat the oven to 375°F. Grease the 24 cups or line them with paper cups.

Soak the raisins and apples in the rum. In a medium bowl, stir the flour, baking powder, and spices together. In a small bowl, combine the milk and vanilla.

In a large bowl, cream the sugar, butter, shortening, and salt together on medium speed for 2 minutes. On low speed, add the eggs one at a time, mixing after each addition. Scrape the sides of the bowl down and continue to mix on medium speed for 2 minutes.

With the mixer on low speed, alternately add the flour and milk mixtures to the creamed ingredients by thirds. Scrape down the sides of the bowl and mix for 1 minute on low speed. Scrape the bowl again, then mix the batter on medium speed for an additional 2 minutes. Fold in the fruit and rum.

Fill the muffin tins three-fourths full and sprinkle liberally with the streusel topping. Bake for 18 to 25 minutes, or until the muffins are golden brown and a toothpick comes out clean when inserted in the center.

Let cool in the pan for 5 minutes before turning the muffins out onto wire racks to cool.

STREUSEL TOPPING

MAKES 3½ CUPS

½ cup (1 stick) butter at room temperature
½ cup packed brown sugar
½ cup wheat bran
1 cup oats
½ cup wheat germ
½ cup walnuts, chopped
¼ cup all-purpose flour
⅛ teaspoon salt

In a medium bowl, blend all the ingredients together. Use now, or cover and refrigerate for up to 3 days.

CHOCOLATE-HAZELNUT BISCOTTI

MAKES 5 DOZEN BISCOTTI

2½ cups all-purpose flour
Pinch of salt
½ cup unsweetened cocoa powder
½ teaspoon baking soda
¾ teaspoon baking powder
4 eggs
1¼ cups sugar
1 teaspoon aniseed
1 cup (5 ounces) hazelnuts, toasted and skinned (see page 13)
1 egg
1 tablespoon water

Preheat the oven to 350°F. Line a baking sheet with parchment paper or grease it. In a medium bowl, stir the flour, salt, cocoa, baking soda, and baking powder together.

In a large bowl, beat the eggs until blended. Stir in the sugar. Add the aniseed and flour mixture and stir to make a soft dough.

Divide the dough in half. On a lightly floured board, pat out each half of dough to form a 6-inch square. Scatter the hazelnuts over each square and push them into the dough. Roll each square into a flattened log about 2 inches wide and 12 to 15 inches long. Beat the egg with the water to make the egg wash. Brush each log with the egg wash.

Bake the biscotti until they are firm to the touch, about 20 minutes. Remove from the oven, leaving the oven on. Transfer the biscotti to a cutting board and let cool for several minutes. Using a large serrated knife, cut the logs into ½-inch-thick diagonal slices. Return to the oven and bake for 10 minutes. Turn the slices over and bake for 10 minutes. Let cool on wire racks. Store in an airtight container.

KEY LIME PIE

Fresh Key limes, which are more yellow than green in color, may be difficult to locate in your area. Fortunately, bottled Key lime juice is widely available.

MAKES ONE 9-INCH PIE; SERVES 8 TO 10

CRUST
½ teaspoon freshly grated nutmeg
½ teaspoon ground cinnamon
1½ cups graham cracker crumbs (about 12 crackers)
¼ cup sugar
4 tablespoons butter, melted

FILLING
4 egg yolks
1 can (14 ounces) sweetened condensed milk
½ cup Key lime juice
Grated zest of 2 Persian limes
Sweetened whipped cream for topping (optional)

TO MAKE THE CRUST: Preheat the oven to 350°F. In a small dry skillet, stir the spices with a wooden spoon until their aroma is apparent. In a medium bowl, combine the spices with the remaining pie crust ingredients and mix until thoroughly combined. Carefully press the mixture into the bottom and sides of a 9-inch pie plate. Form an attractive border around the edges. Bake for 6 to 8 minutes, or until the sides begin to lightly brown. Let cool. Leave the oven at the same temperature.

TO MAKE THE FILLING: In a large bowl, whisk together the egg yolks and condensed milk. Gradually whisk in the lime juice and beat until smooth. Stir in the zest, then carefully pour the pie filling into the baked pie crust and bake for 12 minutes, or until the filling is just set. Let cool.

Place a piece of plastic wrap directly on the surface of the pie to prevent a skin from forming. Refrigerate overnight. Decorate with sweetened whipped cream, if you like.

AMERICAN BOUNTY COBBLER

Cobblers are a favorite American dessert that varies from region to region. Ours has a moist, delicious cake topping.

SERVES 8

3 pounds seasonal fruit, peeled, cored or pitted,
*   and sliced as necessary*
1 cup sugar
¼ teaspoon ground cinnamon
⅛ teaspoon ground nutmeg

TOPPING
3 cups all-purpose flour
2 teaspoons baking powder
2 cups sugar
5 eggs
2 cups milk
1 teaspoon vanilla extract
2 teaspoons grated lemon zest
Ice cream for serving (optional)

Preheat the oven to 350°F. Grease a 9-by-13-inch baking dish.

Put the fruit in a large bowl. In a small bowl, stir together the sugar, cinnamon, and nutmeg. Scatter this mixture over the fruit and toss until the fruit is evenly coated. Let sit for at least 20 minutes while preparing the topping.

TO MAKE THE TOPPING: In a large bowl, stir together the flour, baking powder, and sugar. In a medium bowl, beat the eggs. Whisk in the milk, vanilla extract, and lemon zest. Stir this mixture gradually into the dry ingredients to form a smooth batter.

Ladle the fruit into the prepared baking dish. Spoon or ladle the batter over the fruit. Bake for about 30 minutes, or until the topping is brown and springs back when touched.

Serve with ice cream, if you like.

CRANBERRY-PEAR TART

Fresh cranberries are widely available October through December. Be sure to include this dessert in your holiday menus. In summer, replace the cranberries with fresh blueberries or cherries.

MAKES ONE 10-INCH TART; SERVES 10 TO 12

Pâte Brisée (see page 111)
2 large eggs
½ cup sugar
⅛ teaspoon salt
½ cup (1 stick) butter
2 tablespoons fresh lemon juice
1 teaspoon chocolate extract
¼ cup all-purpose flour
2 large Bartlett pears, peeled, cored, and cut into ½-inch slices
1 cup cranberries

Preheat the oven to 350°F. On a lightly floured board, roll the pâte brisée into a circle ⅛ inch thick. Fit the pastry into a 10-inch tart pan with a removable bottom. Trim the pastry by running the rolling pin over the edges. Generously prick the bottoms and sides of the dough with a fork. Line the pastry with parchment or waxed paper and fill it with pie weights or dried beans. Bake for 20 minutes, or until the edges are set and dry. Remove the weights or beans and paper and bake for 5 to 7 minutes, or until golden brown. Let cool completely.

In a medium bowl, combine the eggs, sugar, and salt. Beat on medium speed until the mixture is thick and pale in color.

In a small, heavy saucepan, melt the butter over medium heat and continue cooking until it turns light brown. Remove from heat and add the lemon juice to stop the cooking process. Immediately strain the butter into the egg mixture and stir it until blended. Stir in the chocolate extract, flour, and cranberries.

Line the pastry shell with the pears. Pour the batter over the fruit and bake for 50 to 60 minutes, or until the fruit is tender and a crisp crust has formed on top. Serve warm or at room temperature.

TARTE TATIN

Treat this peasant-style French dessert like royalty by crowning it either with rich crème fraîche or vanilla ice cream.

MAKES ONE 10-INCH TART; SERVES 10 TO 12

1 cup granulated sugar
½ cup packed light brown sugar
3 thin lime slices
1 vanilla bean, halved lengthwise
½ teaspoon ground cinnamon
About 11 Golden Delicious apples, peeled, halved, and cored
Pâte Brisée (recipe follows)

Generously butter one 10-inch cake pan. Preheat the oven to 425°F.

In a small, heavy skillet, heat the sugar over medium heat until it melts and becomes a deep golden brown. Pour it into the bottom of the cake pan. Let cool, then sprinkle the brown sugar on top of the caramelized sugar. Place the lime slices and vanilla bean on top of the sugar. Dust with cinnamon. Pack the apples tightly in the cake pan.

On a lightly floured board, roll the pâte brisée into a circle ⅛ inch thick. Lay the dough over the apples and use a spatula to tuck the dough in around the edges. Bake the tart for 60 minutes, or until golden brown. Drain the juice from the tart and turn the tart out onto a large plate. Remove the lime and vanilla bean before serving. Serve warm.

CHEFS TIP: If you like, you can cook the excess juice to reduce it, then thicken slightly with cornstarch and use to glaze the apples.

PÂTE BRISÉE

MAKES ONE 10-INCH PASTRY CRUST

2¾ cups sifted cake flour
⅔ cup (1½ sticks) cold butter, cut into small pieces
½ teaspoon salt
½ teaspoon sugar
1½ to 2 tablespoons cold water
1 egg yolk, beaten

In a large bowl, combine the flour and butter. Rub the butter into the pastry flour with your fingers until it resembles coarse meal.

In a small bowl, dissolve the salt and sugar in the water. Gradually stir the egg yolk and water mixture into the flour mixture just until the dough pulls away from the side of the bowl.

On a lightly floured board, form the dough into a ball, then flatten into a disk. Wrap in plastic wrap and refrigerate for at least 30 minutes or up to 2 days . Let sit at room temperature for 15 minutes before rolling out.

CHOCOLATE-ESPRESSO TART

Here, America's favorite flavor is combined with espresso in a crisp cookie crust.

MAKES ONE 10-INCH TART; SERVES 10 TO 12

CRUST
½ cup (1 stick) unsalted butter at room temperature
¼ cup sugar
1 egg yolk
1 teaspoon vanilla extract
¼ teaspoon finely ground espresso
½ teaspoon ground cinnamon
1⅓ cups all-purpose flour

FILLING
1 cup heavy cream
1 teaspoon finely ground espresso
¼ teaspoon ground cinnamon
8 ounces semisweet chocolate, chopped
½ cup (1 stick) unsalted butter, cut into small pieces
3 ounces white chocolate, chopped

GARNISH
Cocoa powder for dusting
Whipped cream

TO MAKE THE CRUST: In a medium bowl, cream the butter and sugar together until smooth.

Add the egg yolk and vanilla and mix for 3 minutes. Add the espresso, cinnamon, and flour, and mix until a soft dough forms. Cover and refrigerate for at least 2 hours, or overnight.

On a lightly floured board, knead the dough just until it is a malleable enough to roll. Roll the dough into a circle ¼ inch thick. Transfer the dough to a 10-inch fluted tart pan with a removable bottom. Gently press the dough into the corners and sides of the pan. Run the rolling pin over the edges of the pan to trim away any excess. Refrigerate the dough for at least 30 minutes.

Preheat the oven to 350°F. Line the tart shell with waxed or parchment paper and fill with pie weights or dried beans. Bake for 15 to 20 minutes, or until lightly golden (rotate the pan if it begins to color unevenly). Remove the weights or beans and let the crust cool completely in the pan. Transfer to a cardboard circle, serving tray, or platter.

TO MAKE THE FILLING: In a small, heavy saucepan, bring the cream to a boil. Add the espresso and cinnamon. Cover and remove from heat. Let sit for 5 minutes. Put the chopped chocolate in a medium bowl. Return the cream to a boil and immediately pour it over the chocolate. Using a whisk, stir slowly until all the chocolate is melted. If necessary, set the bowl over a pan of barely simmering water to completely melt the chocolate. Add the butter and continue to stir until it is melted.

Pour the warm chocolate mixture into the tart shell and spread with a narrow rubber spatula to coat the shell evenly.

In a small saucepan, melt the white chocolate over barely simmering water. Place the warm white chocolate in a pastry bag fitted with a small plain tip. Working from the center of the tart out to the edges, pipe a spiral. Drag the tip of a knife through the spiral to create a design.

Refrigerate the tart for at least 30 minutes. Let sit at room temperature for 1 hour before serving. Sprinkle the tart with cocoa powder and serve each slice with whipped cream.

CHEF'S TIP: Warm a knife in hot water to cut the tart smoothly.

L I N Z E R T O R T E

A good quality raspberry jam is an absolute necessity for this classic torte.

MAKES ONE 10-INCH TORTE; SERVES 10 TO 12

1 cup hazelnuts, toasted, skinned, and chopped (see page 13)
3 cups cake flour
1 teaspoon ground cinnamon
1 teaspoon baking powder
1 cup (2 sticks) unsalted butter at room temperature
¼ cup granulated sugar
1 egg
1 teaspoon vanilla extract
¾ cup seedless or sieved raspberry jam
Powdered sugar for dusting

Preheat the oven to 350°F. Butter and lightly flour a 10-inch round cake or tart pan with a nonremovable bottom.

In a blender or food processor, grind the nuts to a fine powder. Sift the cake flour, cinnamon, and baking powder together. Add the ground hazelnuts to the sifted dry ingredients and set aside.

In a large bowl, cream the butter and sugar together until smooth and fluffy. Mix in the egg and vanilla extract, scraping the sides of the bowl as necessary. Add the dry ingredients and mix until just incorporated. Be careful not to overmix.

Spread half the mixture evenly over the bottom of the prepared pan. Spread the raspberry jam over the mixture to within ½ inch of the edge of the pan.

Transfer the remaining batter to a pastry bag fitted with a No. 6 straight tip and pipe a lattice top and shell border around the edge. Bake the cake for 45 to 50 minutes, or until the crust is crisp and browned. Let cool completely. Dust with powdered sugar before serving.

R A S P B E R R Y S H O R T B R E A D T A R T

This beautiful tart is sure to become a favorite among your family and friends.

MAKES ONE 10-INCH TART; SERVES 10 TO12

C R U S T
½ cup (1 stick) unsalted butter at room temperature
¼ cup granulated sugar
1 egg yolk
¼ teaspoon vanilla extract
1⅓ cups all-purpose flour

F I L L I N G
1 cup crème fraîche
2 tablespoons powdered sugar
1 teaspoon vanilla extract
4 cups fresh raspberries
2 tablespoons honey

TO MAKE THE CRUST: In a large bowl, cream the butter and sugar together until smooth and fluffy. Add the egg yolk and vanilla and continue to mix for 3 more minutes. Add the flour and mix until a soft dough forms. Cover and refrigerate for at least 2 hours or overnight.

On a lightly floured board, knead the dough just until it is malleable enough to roll. Roll the dough into a circle ¼ inch thick Transfer the dough to 10-inch round fluted tart pan with a removable bottom. Gently press the dough into the corners and sides of the pan. Run the rolling pin over the edges of the pan to trim away any excess. Refrigerate the dough for at least 30 minutes.

Preheat the oven to 350°F. Prick the sides and bottom of the tart shell with a fork. Line the shell with waxed or parchment paper and fill with pie weights or dried beans. Bake for 15 to 20 minutes, or until lightly golden (rotate the pan if it begins to color unevenly). Let cool completely in the pan. Transfer to a cardboard circle, serving tray, or platter.

In a deep bowl, whip the crème fraîche, powdered sugar, and vanilla to stiff peaks.

Spread this mixture in an even layer in the cooled tart shell.

Carefully arrange the raspberries over the filling, placing them so they completely cover the filling. Drizzle the honey over the tart just before serving.

PEAR SKILLET CAKE

Other fruits, such as peaches, plums, and pineapple, may also be used in this recipe. When unmolded, this dessert will resemble a tarte tatin, but it has only a fraction of the fat and calories.

MAKES ONE 10-INCH CAKE; SERVES 12

2 cups cake flour
2¼ teaspoons baking powder
½ teaspoon baking soda
½ teaspoon salt
1 tablespoon ground ginger
2 teaspoons ground cinnamon
¼ teaspoon ground nutmeg
¼ teaspoon ground mace
¼ cup ground allspice
2 Bartlett pears
2 egg yolks

¼ cup molasses
⅓ cup honey
¼ cup hot water
3 egg whites
1 tablespoon unsalted butter
½ cup packed brown sugar
48 candied walnut halves (see Chef's Tip)
Vanilla ice cream or frozen yogurt for serving (optional)

Preheat the oven to 350°F. Sift the flour, baking powder, baking soda, salt, ginger, cinnamon, nutmeg, mace, and allspice together into a medium bowl. Set aside.

Peel, core, and grate one of the pears. In a small bowl, combine the egg yolks, molasses, honey, and grated pear and stir until blended. Add the hot water and stir until the honey and molasses are evenly blended. Stir the wet ingredients into the dry ingredients. In a large bowl, whip the egg whites to stiff, glossy peaks and fold them into the pear batter.

In a 10-inch ovenproof skillet, melt the butter over medium-high heat. Add the brown sugar and cook until it darkens slightly. Remove from heat. Peel, core, and slice the remaining pear. Arrange the pear slices in the skillet in a spiral shape.

Pour the batter over the pears and bake for 20 minutes, or until the cake springs back when lightly touched. Turn the cake out onto a parchment-lined baking sheet. Let the cake cool slightly before slicing and serving. Garnish each portion with candied walnuts. Serve with ice cream or frozen yogurt, if you like.

CHEF'S TIP: Candied walnuts can be found in your local grocer's baking section.

WARM LEMON PUDDING CAKES WITH WARM FRUIT AND CUSTARD SAUCE

SERVES 12

2 tablespoons butter at room temperature
1¼ cups sugar
¼ teaspoon salt
6 egg yolks
½ cup all-purpose flour
4 teaspoons grated lemon zest
½ cup fresh lemon juice
2 cups milk
8 egg whites
Custard Sauce (recipe follows)
Poached Dried Fruit (see page 103)

Preheat the oven to 350°F. Liberally butter 12 small ramekins or custard cups and dust with granulated sugar. Place 3 layers of paper towels in the bottom of a shallow baking dish. Set the ramekins or cups in the pan.

In a large bowl, cream the butter, sugar, and salt together until smooth. Beat in the egg yolks. Scrape down the sides of the bowl to blend the batter properly. Add the flour and mix until smooth. Stir in the lemon zest and juice. Add the milk and mix thoroughly.

In a large bowl, beat the egg whites until stiff glossy peaks form. Fold into the batter.

Ladle the batter into the ramekins or cups. Carefully pour boiling water around the ramekins or cups to reach halfway up the sides. Bake the pudding cakes until they are set and the center springs back when lightly pressed, about 30 minutes. Let sit in the water bath for 10 minutes to finish cooking.

Serve the warm pudding with custard sauce and poached fruit.

CUSTARD SAUCE

MAKES 4 CUPS

2 cups milk
2 cups heavy cream
½ vanilla bean, split lengthwise, or 1 teaspoon vanilla extract
1 cup sugar
8 egg yolks

In a large, heavy saucepan, combine the milk, cream, vanilla bean or extract, and ½ cup of the sugar. Mix well and bring to a simmer over medium heat.

In a medium bowl, combine the remaining ½ cup sugar with the egg yolks. Whisk until thoroughly combined. Whisk about ½ cup of the hot milk mixture into the egg yolks. Gradually whisk in 1 more cup. Whisk the yolk mixture into the hot milk. Gently cook the sauce over low heat until it is thick enough to coat a spoon.

Strain the sauce through a fine-meshed sieve into a bowl set over ice. Stir the sauce as it cools.

CHEF'S TIP: Instead of preparing this sauce, you may melt a good-quality vanilla ice cream in a double boiler. Cover and refrigerate the melted ice cream for at least 1 hour. Stir well before serving.

RIGÓ JANCSI
Chocolate Cream Cake

This traditional Hungarian cake layers a rich chocolate filling between rum-flavored sponge cake slices.

SERVES 8

2¼ cups sifted cake flour
1 teaspoon baking powder
1¼ cups (2½ sticks) unsalted butter at room temperature
⅔ cup sifted powdered sugar
12 eggs, separated, at room temperature
8 ounces semisweet chocolate, melted
2 teaspoons vanilla extract
1½ cups granulated sugar
Rum-Flavored Simple Syrup (recipe follows)
Chocolate Cream Filling (recipe follows)

Preheat the oven to 375°F. Line a 15-by-10-inch jelly roll pan with parchment or grease it. Sift the cake flour and baking powder together twice and set aside.

In a large bowl, cream the butter and powdered sugar together until very light and fluffy. Add the egg yolks one at a time until all are incorporated, scraping the bowl periodically with a rubber spatula. Fold the melted chocolate and vanilla extract into the egg mixture until fully incorporated.

In a large bowl, whip the egg whites until frothy. Gradually beat in the granulated sugar to form stiff, glossy peaks. Stir one third of the meringue into the chocolate mixture to lighten it, then fold in the remaining meringue.

Fold the flour mixture into the chocolate mixture in fourths, until just blended. Spread the batter as evenly as possible in the prepared pan. Bake the cake for about 12 minutes, or until a toothpick inserted near the center of the cake comes out clean.

Let cool in the pan, then remove to a cutting board. Cut the cake into three 5-by-10-inch strips. Brush all sides of each strip with the rum syrup. Spread the chocolate cream on top of the bottom and middle layers and stack into a 3-layer cake. Refrigerate for at least 2 hours before serving.

CHEF'S TIP: For an alcohol-free version of this cake, replace the rum in the syrup and the cream filling with an equal amount of brewed espresso.

RUM-FLAVORED SIMPLE SYRUP

MAKES ½ CUP

¼ cup sugar
¼ cup water
2 tablespoons dark rum

In a small saucepan, combine the sugar and water. Bring to a boil. Remove from heat and let cool to room temperature. Stir in the rum.

CHOCOLATE CREAM FILLING

MAKES 2 CUPS

12 ounces semisweet chocolate, chopped
½ cup heavy cream
1 teaspoon vanilla extract
1 tablespoon dark rum

Melt the chocolate in a double boiler over barely simmering water. Set aside and keep warm. In a deep bowl, beat the heavy cream just until very soft peaks form. Stir in the vanilla extract and dark rum.

Spoon one third of the whipped cream on top of the chocolate. Quickly whisk the cream into the chocolate together to form a smooth paste. Fold in the remaining two thirds of the cream.

ESPRESSO-CHOCOLATE CAKES WITH COFFEE BEAN CRISPS

SERVES 8

6 tablespoons brewed espresso
¾ cup granulated sugar
9 ounces bittersweet chocolate, chopped
¾ cup (1½ sticks) unsalted butter, melted
4 eggs
Powdered sugar for dusting
Coffee Bean Crisps (recipe follows)

Preheat the oven to 350°F. Set each of eight 3-inch cake rings in the center of a 6-inch square of aluminum foil. Pleat the foil up around the sides of the ring. Set the rings in a large, shallow baking dish.

In a small saucepan, bring the espresso and ½ cup of the sugar to a boil. Remove from heat and stir in the chocolate until melted. Add the butter and stir until completely blended. Set aside at room temperature.

In a medium bowl, beat the eggs and the remaining ¼ cup sugar until pale in color. Fold the chocolate mixture into the beaten eggs. Divide this batter evenly among the cake rings.

Pour hot water into the baking dish to come halfway up the sides of the rings. Bake for 30 minutes, or until the top of the cakes feel firm.

Let cool to room temperature, then refrigerate for at least 1 hour and preferably overnight. Unmold and arrange each cake on a chilled dessert plate. Dust with powdered sugar and serve with a coffee bean crisp.

COFFEE BEAN CRISPS

MAKES 16 COOKIES

2 tablespoons coffee beans
¾ cup (1½ sticks) plus 2 tablespoons unsalted butter
¾ cup sugar
3 tablespoons light corn syrup
¼ cup heavy cream or more as needed
2 cups (8 ounces) sliced blanched almonds

Preheat the oven to 375°F. Line a baking sheet with parchment paper or grease it. Use a rolling pin to finely crush the coffee beans. Set aside.

In a medium, heavy saucepan, bring the butter, sugar, corn syrup, and cream to a boil. Stir in the almonds and coffee beans. Cook over medium heat, stirring constantly, for 3 minutes. Remove from heat.

Bake a spoonful of the batter on a sheet pan lined with parchment paper to test its consistency. If it spreads out too thin, return it to heat and cook the batter a little longer. If the mixture is too thick, stir in a tablespoon or two of heavy cream over low heat. Test the batter again and make any adjustments necessary.

Using a wet tablespoon, spoon equal portions of the batter onto the prepared baking sheet, spacing them 5 inches apart. Flatten each spoonful into a circle 4 inches in diameter. (Wet the spoon as necessary to keep the batter from sticking.)

Bake in the center of the oven until light brown, about 10 minutes. Quickly cut the warm cookies into crescent shapes using round cookie cutters. Using a metal spatula, transfer the crescents to a wire rack to cool. Repeat until all the batter is used. Store in an airtight container for up to 2 weeks.

TORTA DI NOCCIOLE CON RICOTTA E CIOCCOLATA

Hazelnut Torte with Ricotta and Chocolate
....

MAKES ONE 10-INCH CAKE; SERVES 10 TO 12

3 cups cake flour
½ cup cornstarch
2 cups heavy cream
2 pounds semisweet chocolate, chopped
12 eggs
1½ cups granulated sugar
4 tablespoons butter, melted and cooled to room temperature
2 pounds ricotta cheese
1¼ cups hazelnuts, toasted, skinned, and coarsely chopped
   (see page 13)
¾ cup powdered sugar, sifted
¼ cup brewed espresso
Lightly whipped cream for serving

Preheat the oven to 350°F. Lightly grease and flour a 10-inch cake pan. Sift the cake flour and cornstarch together twice and set aside.

In a double boiler over barely simmering water, heat the heavy cream with the chocolate. Stir until evenly blended. Let cool to room temperature.

In another double boiler over barely simmering water, whisk the eggs and sugar together until the mixture is lukewarm. Remove from heat and beat until the mixture falls in a thick, slowly dissolving ribbon from the beater.

Fold the dry ingredients into the egg mixture. Fold the butter into the batter. Pour into the prepared pan. Bake for 25 to 30 minutes, or until the cake is springy to the touch. Let cool in the pan or on a wire rack for 10 minutes. Unmold the cake and let cool on a wire rack.

Mix the ricotta, hazelnuts, and powdered sugar together.

Place cake on a cutting board. Holding a knife parallel to the board, cut the cake into 3 equal layers and sprinkle each with the espresso. Spread half of the ricotta mixture on top of one layer. Top with a second layer and spread with the remaining mixture. Top with the third layer.

Spread the chocolate mixture evenly over the top and sides of the cake. Allow to set until firm. Serve cut into slices, garnished with whipped cream.

CHOCOLATE SOUFFLÉ CAKE

MAKES ONE 8-INCH CAKE; SERVES 8 TO 10

11 ounces bittersweet chocolate, chopped
4 tablespoons butter
1 egg
7 egg yolks
½ cup sugar
¼ cup Grand Marnier (optional)
7 egg whites

Preheat the oven to 350°F. Line the bottom of an 8-inch round cake pan with parchment paper and the sides with a paper collar. Butter the paper well.

In a double boiler over barely simmering water, stir the chocolate and butter together until completely melted. Set aside.

In a medium bowl, beat the egg, egg yolks, and ¼ cup of the sugar together on high speed for 3 to 5 minutes, until it is tripled in volume and soft peaks form. Gently stir in the liqueur, if you like. Set aside.

In a large bowl, beat the egg whites and remaining sugar until soft peaks form. Fold the chocolate mixture into the yolks, then fold in the egg whites. Pour the batter into the prepared cake pan and bake for 50 minutes, or until a toothpick inserted in the center comes out clean.

Cool on a wire rack. Loosen the edges with a knife and unmold unto a cake plate. Cool completely, slice, and serve.

TABLE OF EQUIVALENTS

The exact equivalents in the following tables have been rounded for convenience.

LIQUID AND DRY MEASURES

U.S.	METRIC
¼ teaspoon	1.25 milliliters
½ teaspoon	2.5 milliliters
1 teaspoon	5 milliliters
1 tablespoon (3 teaspoons)	15 milliliters
1 fluid ounce (2 tablespoons)	30 milliliters
¼ cup	60 milliliters
⅓ cup	80 milliliters
1 cup	240 milliliters
1 pint (2 cups)	480 milliliters
1 quart (4 cups, 32 ounces)	960 milliliters
1 gallon (4 quarts)	3.84 liters
1 ounce (by weight)	28 grams
¼ pound (4 ounces)	114 grams
1 pound	454 grams
2.2 pounds	1 kilogram

OVEN TEMPERATURES

FAHRENHEIT	CELSIUS	GAS
250	120	½
275	140	1
300	150	2
325	160	3
350	180	4
375	190	5
400	200	6
425	220	7
450	230	8
475	240	9
500	260	10

LENGTH MEASURES

⅛ inch	3 millimeters
¼ inch	6 millimeters
½ inch	12 millimeters
1 inch	2.5 centimeters